Surviving The Micronova

This Train Is On The Tracks

Book 2 in the Quantum Dream Series

by allen aslan heart

Copyright © 2022 allen aslan heart

All rights reserved. No part of this book may be reproduced in any form or by any electronic or mechanical means including information and retrieval systems without prior permission from the publisher in writing.

Library of Congress Cataloging-in-Publication Data
Heart, Allen Aslan, 1941-
Surviving The Micronova: This Train Is On The Tracks
/ allen aslan heart. First Edition.

Book 2 of the Quantum Dream Series

ISBN Paperback: 9798885440097
ISBN eBook: 9798885440196
ISBN Hardcover: 9798885440202

Cover and Interior Artwork: AHONU.com
Manuscript Editor: AHONU
Manuscript Designer: AHONU.com

Published in the USA

Address all inquiries to:
World of Empowerment
an imprint of **Twin Flame Productions LLC**
Via eMail to admin@twinflameproductions.us
Or phone +1-224-588-8026

https://twinflameproduction.us

Warning—Limits of Liability and Disclaimer of Warranty
The author and publisher shall not be liable for your misuse of the material in this book. This book is strictly for informational, educational and entertainment purposes only. The author and/or publisher do not guarantee or warrant that anyone following the techniques, suggestions, tips, ideas, or strategies in this book will become successful at anything. The opinions of the author are not necessarily those of the publisher. The author and/or publisher shall have neither liability nor responsibility to anyone with respect to any loss or damage howsoever caused, or alleged to be caused, directly or indirectly by the information contained in this book. Always consult a licensed health practitioner for all health issues.

SURVIVING THE MICRONOVA
This Train Is On The Tracks

*This is for those WHO have eyes to see,
for those WHO have ears to hear,
WHO faintly recall WHO they really Are
and now would remember another world backstage.*

allen heart

Christianity

In my 1st book, *Dancing a Quantum Dream* (https://amzn.to/36qGSaF), I warned **the train is on the tracks**. That was a strange thing to say, but within the next few decades, we will see a micronova of our Sun, reversal of our magnetosphere, unlocking of the crust and/or tilt of the Earth, tsunamis that sweep across continents, major earthquakes and volcanoes, and the extinction of 10-50% of species. Human civilization will be hard hit because of our extreme dependence on technology, especially electricity.

This book, *Surviving The Micronova: This Train Is On The Tracks*, is critical for this time. The North Pole is nearly in Siberia, headed for the Bay of Bengal. The South Pole has left Antarctica, headed north. The First Horseman Of The Apocalypse is in the sky (the brilliant white sun). Next, it will turn red, then black. At that point, you have 17 hours to seek shelter. Some experts say it will happen in the next decade or two. Time enough for you to prepare... or not.

The increase in interstellar dust signals that we are now in the Galactic Current Sheet. The outer planets have already started their journey through it. Pluto has lost its atmosphere, the weather on Neptune has reversed, there are winds in the red spot of Jupiter, X-rays and radio signals on

Mars show increased seismic activity, and winds on Venus have increased. Our Sun has begun the initial stages leading to the accumulation of a shell that will eventually be blasted our way in a micronova. The magnetosphere of the sun is changing, increasing helium in the corona and solar wind.

Nearby stars that follow us in the journey, Proxima Centauri and Barnards have flared, or become more active. The signs of the heavens tell us we weren't here for the last one 12,000 years ago, but we will get a close up and personal experience this time. We will understand their telling of their stories from the time of Göbekli Tepe at the beginning of the current human civilization.

My poetry is Gnostic. I've used it to unfold Gnosticism, the original Christian teachings from the 1st Century before it became the church of empire and went politically ape in the quest for power, with inquisition, murder, genocide, and deicide. The church made it necessary to hide documents in vases in the desert. But my focus is on the secrets that were never intended to be secrets, hidden in plain sight.

WHO we are is Consciousness of God before we chose to be born into this 4D world to experience consciously, and when the body, our vehicle, is disabled and inoperative, we return to pure consciousness for the rest of eternity. That I am affirming in poetry, quantum physics, and lucid learning through shamanic drumming, meditation, and T'ai Chi in preparation for the cataclysm that awaits us. We have survived several of these and with necessary preparation, we can do so again.

WE, our consciousness, is the Holy Spirit that completes the creation by manifesting the reality that heaven only projects as energetic waves. Our consciousness was found to be essential for waves to become particles—for potentiality of creation to become the reality of creation requires an 'intelligent observer'.

From the dawn of creation we are co-creators, as I was led to write in my poetry, not really aware of that significance. Science discovered this a century ago, and no one has picked up on its significance. Einstein grumbled that he preferred to think the moon is shining even if he's not looking. Then came the near-death experiences that gave us a new look at our true nature. I was given the WHO-WHAT sutras to make it clear that our consciousness precedes our birth.

WE, our consciousness, play in the WHAT that was born, so that we, creation, can evolve through direct experience. Our consciousness is eternal from the dawn of creation, our bodies are not. Our natural home is heaven! When I close my eyes in sleep, consciousness is free to wander, and sometimes I remember the dream. When my body awakens, my consciousness is there on the ready for another day of experiencing the magic of God's creation. Sometimes, when I listen, I can hear the whispers of others beyond the realm who animate my imagination from a world beyond the body and its limitations. I call those others the Grandmothers and Grandfathers. The communication is possible through the heart, which is far more than a pump—it is our entry point to the other world.

allen aslan heart ~ whiteaglesoaring

Table of Contents

Introduction	1
Now What? Dancing With A Star	10
Quantum Heaven	22
Earth Dream Theater	25
A Window To Consciousness	27
The Physics Of Co-Creation	39
Come World	42
What Is Consciousness?	46
Smudging And The Sage Ceremony	59
Shamanic Drumming	64
Care Of The Drum	72
Listening To Whispers	77
The Now Moment	78
Shamanic/Gnostic Poetry	82
WHO I AM Is More Than What…	102
Meditation Basics	114
Meditation Through The Hearts Code	129
T'ai Chi For The Heart	138
Surviving The Micronova	152
Practical Survival	159
Food For Survival	165
Growing Your Own	177
Thank You For Reading!	184
Acknowledgements	186
About The Author	191
Bibliography	192

Introduction

At the end of my first book, *Dancing a Quantum Dream —An 80 Year Journey of Initiation, Quiet Miracles, Teaching and Shamanic Communications*, I warned that **the train is on the tracks**. After I sent the manuscript to my publishers, I felt I had perhaps overlooked that foreboding warning. I had only examined that topic in an intellectual, disinterested scientific demeanor, typical in our age of materialism, intellectualizing our experiences.

After all, that was how I was raised in the 50's, on a farm in Minnesota. When I questioned that, soon I was shown that the train was, indeed real, and we are on the tracks. Soon, my guides led me to search for answers for that open-ended query. I found we are nearing the end of a recurring micronova cycle that was barely suggested to me about 7 decades ago when I found three books by Immanuel Velikovsky in the county library—*Worlds in Collision, Ages In Chaos,* and *Earth in Upheaval.* The works of DeLuc and Cuvier, catastrophe and cataclysm, were an early part of my literary life along with the science fiction of Clifford Simak, Isaac Asimov, Robert Heinlein, and Arthur C. Clarke.

Only in examining my life experiences in writing my first book, did I see the significance and association of the collection of memories and anecdotes. I realized I had been led on a lifelong shamanic-gnostic adventure without knowing what all that meant. After all, I was just a farm kid from Minnesota, what did I know? Who knows! Looking back, I saw that little hints were dropped along the way. Hints that I didn't connect until enough were experienced, but filed away as just weird, if somewhat interesting.

Within the next few decades, we will see a micronova of our Sun, reversal of our magnetosphere, unlocking of the crust and/or tilt of the Earth, tsunamis that sweep across continents, major Earthquakes and volcanoes, and the extinction of 10-50% of species. Human civilization will be hard hit because of our vulnerability due to our extreme dependence on technology, especially electricity.[OS 58]

Are there other clues that something is about to happen? Shouldn't we see magnetic changes on other planets in our solar system, or other stars in our galaxy? We got a report from NASA's Mars Insight Lander that it had detected more than 300 MarsQuakes. Reports from Venus revealed the winds are getting ⅓ faster, and now we've found our sister planets that have already started into the Galactic Current Sheet are showing its effects, such as the collapse of the atmosphere on Pluto, and a reversal of weather patterns on Neptune.[OS 75] This signals that any of the planets moving through the Galactic Current Sheet might have weather systems reversed, or collapsed. Winds in Jupiter's Great Red Spot and on Venus are speeding up. Jupiter is giving off radio signals from the Red Spot. Saturn, Uranus, and Neptune have had strange superstorms in their atmospheres, and auroras have increased on Uranus.[OS 75-76]

In addition to the 12,000-year cycle micronova, we are already in a 6,000-year cycle, called a Heinrich event, that manifests with magnetic changes and a shift in the hydroclimate. These are now happening, and still ahead, an uptick in volcanoes which we have not yet seen.[OS 59]

We are on the harmonic, the 12,000-year cycle that will mesh with the 6,000-year Heinrich event that started in 1859 with the Carrington event. Every 6,000 years there is an amplified, more extreme Heinrich event. In addition to the others that are part of the 12,000-year micronova, a superflare can be 100x greater than the Carrington event.[OS 25]

In the last few years two new kinds of nova and a new type of star were discovered! New types of nova events! Nova with no ejections! Without binaries! No luminosity! So much has happened in recent years that you would have to be reading the peer-reviewed literature to know the possibilities for nova can be found all around our star. The solar nova has become possible within the known nova events in the Milky Way Galaxy.[OS 99]

We know the stars that are following behind as we travel through the Galactic Current Sheet are also showing their own nova event. Planets and stars are affected by their journey through the Galactic Current Sheet. Proxima Centauri has been carefully observed for years and well-established as a star that flares, its range of flare limits well-established—and then it had a superflare. Barnard's star was thought to be inactive and then it began flaring.[NEW 90] Astrophysicists have found the X-ray-inflated local bubble of hot gas surrounding our solar system from previous micronovas, and our solar system is in the exact center.[OS 98]

A major update came from the Chinese lunar lander that also found the glassy spherules even larger than those found by our Apollo program.[OS 91] Earth's speed of rotation is increasing each year. In 2020, Earth broke its record for rotational speed several times. 2021 was slightly shorter than usual, and 2022 is expected to set new records for the fastest year and shortest day.[OS 92]

Mulligan and Koren, psychologists in Canada, published their study, *Geopsychology Of Instrumental Aggression: Daily Occurrence Of Global Terrorism And Solar-Magnetic Activity (1970-2018)* in the *Advances In Social Sciences Research Journal* in 2021. They reported emotional instability is more common under magnetic storm conditions and increased cosmic rays.[OS 103] If you wonder why craziness has picked up in frequency, here is at least a partial factor—space weather may exacerbate nascent anger and heighten violence. We should focus on what we must know so we can bolster our chances of surviving this cataclysm, as our ancestors did. We ourselves are ample evidence that this is survivable. We are the family of those survivors of 12,000 years ago. It's in our genes. Besides, we are more than we seem.

The Large Low-Sheer Velocity Provinces (LLSVP) structures in the Mantle suggest the North Magnetic Pole will re-orient itself in the Bay of Bengal, turning much of India into the new Arctic Circle. But since we now know that the crust can and probably will unlock from the underlying mantle, continents can move, some rise and fall, sliding under and over each other.

We finally have the mechanism Einstein was looking for that would unlock the crust from the underlying mantle. Einstein died three years before Hapgood's book was published. He didn't know that the crust can unlock during a recurrent micronova, or that the hyperactivity of Earth's magnetosphere increases the plasticity of rocks at the interface of crust and mantle so that they can unlock.

All that remained was to find what drove the continental plates to move. Einstein only had Greenland's ice mass throwing the Earth out of balance, but there was not enough mass in Greenland's Ice Field to make the crust move. The YouTube channel of Veritasium showed how this could happen—a spinning object weightless in space, jumped from its angle of rotation to another angle of rotation because of asymmetry, then flipped back to its original angle of rotation.

Ben Davidson comments, "This is pretty close to what we are looking for with the Earth." [NEW 57] While this is usually only applicable to asymmetrical objects, The Earth IS asymmetrical because of the LLSVPs, massive pluming branches that extend from the region of the outer core up through the mantle, even penetrating through the crust in places. This asymmetry makes the crust layers break up during a micronova. This is called the Dzhanibekov Effect [https://www.youtube.com/watch?v=1VPfZ_XzisU] but the LLSVP structures inside the Mantle suggest the North Magnetic Pole will re-orient itself in the Bay of Bengal, turning much of India into the new Arctic Circle.

I needed to know the nature of the cataclysm and its time of arrival. Scientists have been monitoring the North Magnetic Pole for over a hundred years. I found a series on consciousness written by Penny Kelly. One of her sources on YouTube, Maverickstar Reloaded, presented information that showed that the North Magnetic Pole had begun to move rapidly from its meandering around northern Canada. The host of Maverickstar Reloaded posited that as the magnetosphere gets weaker, and when the traveling pole gets to the 40-degree point, it will accelerate to Zero Polarity, then it will reverse polarity. This was doubted by Ben Davidson at Suspicious Observers who wrote *The Next End of the World*.

In fact, what we are more likely facing is not a change of magnetic polarity from north to south but a mere moving of the north magnetic pole to a new location, a polar recursion, not a polar reversal, or flip. In a flip, if the flow of plasma energy stops, the rotation of the Earth stops. But there are no brakes to make that stop immediate. Some folks are talking about off-the-chart tsunamis, but even if the Earth is spinning at 1,000 mph at the equator (736 mph at 45°) and the power that makes it spin is switched off and it slowed down at a rate of just 17 mph/minute, the oceans would slow down at about the same rate so there would not be mile high or two-mile-high tsunamis. In a recursion, the poles are eventually at a new location, but the Earth rotation might not stop. Instead, coastal regions might be hit with moderate flooding. Yet, evidence from past events show waves taking out whole continents; perhaps if the crust unlocks, buckles, and continents are swallowed by the abyss.

Under the Antarctic ice there is a flash-frozen tropical rain forest and in the Arctic, there are the remains of tropical coral. Clearly, the poles were once tropical paradises. Dr. Paul Delaney from Toronto's York University says the magnetic pole reversals happen about every half a million years and the last magnetic pole reversal occurred 650,000 years ago, and our magnetosphere has already lost about 9% strength in the last 200 years. The prior reversals occurred more often than that, something like 250,000+ years. Polar recursions, the movement of a pole to another location, happen more often. Continental tsunamis can occur when the crust unlocks and plates of the crust move, slide against, or under each other.

That means the pole movements over the last 650,000 years were ONLY EXCURSIONS and not reversals, and that the North Magnetic Pole wanders away from the North Geographic Pole, but it doesn't flip to south. It moves to a Bay of Bengal location somewhere between India and Indonesia, perhaps between the islands of Java and Sumatra. The South Magnetic Pole eventually organizes somewhere near the coastline of Ecuador and Peru, creating a new Equator running from Antarctica through New Zealand, Fiji Islands, through the Bering Strait, the former North Pole, Norway, Germany, the Swiss Alps, Italy, Tunisia, Libya, Niger, Gabon, Angola, Namibia, bringing drought and desertification.

What that means for India and the Amazon is that the people in warm climates will suddenly be in Arctic climates instead of Tropical, and the Eskimos won't be able to build igloos or hunt seals. Mountains at the new Equator such as the former Antarctic will likely remain cold because of altitude instead of latitude.

A weakening of the Earth's magnetosphere has already led to the beaching of some whales and interfered with the migration of others. Any semblance of a magnetosphere is protective, but none is disaster. The weaker the magnetosphere, the greater our exposure to cosmic rays which will likely damage the electric grid so that serious repair is not possible for many years or decades. A rapidly collapsing pole could contribute to bigger earthquakes. In the past this magnetic interruption caused the Earth's crust to slip—that's why Chicago was once the North Pole.

What looks to be an excursion instead of a 180° reversal means that the Earth's spin takes more of a left turn than a U-turn with the former poles at the equator, and with two of today's equatorial regions rotating at the poles instead. The former North Geographic Pole would become the direction in which the sun sets, and the Northern Lights would show up over the new north poles in the direction that once was called east.

All this and more might happen but nobody really knows what it will be like or how long before it happens. Some say November or December 2023, others between 2030 and 2050. We may have time to prepare.

If the magnetic field around the Earth is disrupted, harmful radiation will reach the surface of the Earth. Where the angle of the incoming radiation is closer to 90°, i.e. equator and the tropics, the temperatures will skyrocket. Without a magnetosphere to shield us from high energy particles, the Earth temperatures will rapidly rise. Combustibles will combust. Then, at some time later, the micronova from our Sun is triggered.

Just under the thin crust is a zone of thermo/electrical plasticity that sticks the bottom of the crust to the top of the mantle, locking the two layers together. Normally, the crust, floating on the mantle, sticks and grips. Changes in temperature or electro-magnetic forces can get them to let go, and the crust unlocked, can float away from its mooring like a boat from a dock. An old-fashioned way of saying continental drift.

With the magnetosphere weakening, reduced protection from the solar wind can bring hydrogen atoms and oxygen together to hypothetically produce 'star water' above our heads. Beyond the clouds, we find an electric layer we call the ionosphere. NASA discovered that large Coronal Mass Ejections (CMEs) from the Sun, cause these layers to produce significant amounts of hydrogen and oxygen, which, meeting in an environment that brings oxygen and hydrogen to produce water ABOVE the clouds, seems like the heavens open up to create a great flood.

Although this hypothesis is developing, it has been shown that solar hydrogen can liberate oxygen trapped in space debris and still have the energy to make water in space. Hydroxyl ions clump and fall to Earth. A weakened magnetosphere=greater penetration of cosmic rays=more cloud particles=star water over and above what the lower clouds might produce in times of solar quiet.

Author and teacher, Penny Kelly also referred to *World's In Collision* by Immanuel Velikovsky which I had read as a kid in Jr. High School. Wow! That lit me up quickly. About a decade ago, I found Velikovsky's book, and I added it to my personal library. Again, too many coincidences to shrug off! I had been warned long ago but the scientific information had been hidden and unavailable for most of my life. Then, when I searched for 'consciousness', I found Penny Kelly's *Consciousness & Energy* 4-Volume set and read her sources. They mentioned the change of the color of the Sun from a merry yellow to a blazing white,[NEW 45] and I knew I needed to take this seriously. A recurring micronova may be in the cards before the end of the decade… or three.

The Spirals sang and danced.
"He has listened to our whispers and songs in the spirit-wind to recognize that there is significance in our repeated warning that there IS a train on the tracks," sang the Grandmothers.
"The nudges from the Seventh Fire Prophecy, the Siberian Elders, and the queries of Graham Hancock and Robert Bauval at the Egyptian pyramid into why the Egyptians built the pyramids, focused his deeper inquiry into the train on the tracks mystery," drummed a Grandfather.
"He had pre-planned a lot of people to help him along the way," danced the Dreamkeeper, "and wrote a lot of poetry for us to feed back to him."
"That was quite a giggle to see him scramble to write down some of those before he forgot them," giggled a glowing sprite.

Now What? Dancing With A Star

While I was living in Vienna, designing, marketing and teaching about my dreamcatchers, I would accompany my friend Hermine to her office to research and write on one of her computers. One day, a woman entered, noticed me, and excitedly began speaking in German. Without a clue what she was saying, I shrugged and went back to continue with whatever task I had set for myself. She quickly walked over to Hermine's desk continuing to look back at me and talking. She and Hermine had a short conversation and she left, staring at me, and talking to herself in German.

I asked Hermine what that was all about. She said her friend had just returned from South America where she had attended an ayahuasca ceremony. The Shaman had offered her an opportunity to do a shamanic journey, which she eagerly accepted. While on her vision quest, she had seen me leading a group under a fiery sky doing ceremony to hold the Earth together while the Earth shook and the heavens rumbled. She was shaken when she saw me calmly sitting at a computer in an office in Vienna. Weird!

I filed that little episode in the weird file and shook my head in disbelief. Years after the Austrian woman was shocked to see me sitting at a computer at her friend's office, I chuckled at that odd revelation of her ayahuasca vision of me holding the Earth together when a friend shared with me about a new company he was joining, Dirt Glue, whose slogan was "Holding the Earth together." I laughed then, but now suddenly it isn't as funny—or is it?

Even before the Civil War, we had the first notice from our Sun to wake up and pay attention. The Earth's magnetic field began to change in 1859, as noted in the Carrington event in which a magnetic storm on the Sun caused an electrical storm on Earth that melted copper telegraph wires and started fires in telegraph stations. It shocked telegraph operators who were able to turn off their equipment and send messages using current induced from the Sun. The Carrington Event was the most intense geomagnetic storm in recorded history, which announced the beginning of the current micronova and Heinrich event with a large coronal mass ejection (CME). Twelve years earlier W. Barlow, chief engineer of the East Midlands Railway, identified an auroral display related to induced electrical currents in telegraph wires. We've been losing magnetic strength in our magnetic field, now down 20-25%, an additional 5-10% lost in the past year. When losses accelerate, the shift will be 100X faster, at which time we have less than 5 years to the reversal of Earth's magnetism. Say hello to a cold snap, as high UV from sunflares melts ice and cools the oceans.[OS 61-62]

At the end of World War II, the United States military in the fog of war had seen the building of a great empire, the Soviet Union, and our government moved quickly to block that happening to us. Our military intelligence wanted to know about the Arctic to avoid a Soviet attack from that region. So, the Strategic Air Command sent one of their officers, Major Maynard E. White, on Project Nanook, a reconnaissance mission to the Arctic in the late 1940s. He found the North Magnetic Pole, and evidence that it had moved, and like Admiral Byrd in Antarctica, found tropical fossils that could only mean the poles had once been in tropical regions. This information was presented in top secret meetings at the Pentagon, attended by Charles Hapgood. Major White saved information from these meetings which was all classified. He went on to direct data collection, running spies in Europe and Africa, and served the Apollo missions communicating with the astronauts in their exploration of the Moon's surface. When he retired, he gave all his papers to his son, Ken, to publish after he died. *World in Peril* was published in 1994.

Major White had found five layers of tropical and polar sediment, separated by 10-12,000 years. Each layer showed evidence of magnetic excursion, which takes place in about one day, driving a deluge and an ice age. The poles return to their original location at the next event.[NEW 13-14]

The US government has known since 1947 that a pending geological event could occur at any time, causing the extinction of many lifeforms, including our own. A train IS on the tracks, and the elite in our government know it's coming. Immanuel Velikovsky had no opportunity to add that information to his book published in 1950. I was in 2nd year of elementary school at the time, and this information was never in any of my schoolbooks. The whole field of catastrophism was subverted so that when I studied Geology and Astronomy, it was not included! Our government withheld it as classified.

Hapgood and Einstein were the first to suggest the unlocking of the crust at the low-velocity zone between the crust and mantle where the two Earth layers stick and grip.[NEW 28] This is probably why Einstein stopped wondering IF the crust moved, just how. The detachment of the crust from the mantle had not yet been associated with the magnetosphere. Einstein wrote the foreword for Hapgood's book on catastrophism but died three years before it was published. Hapgood was originally OSS which later became CIA. Hapgood intentionally squandered Einstein's contribution to his book by totally ignoring the evidence gathered by White's team, making his theory easily debunked. The whole field of catastrophism was derailed for a generation and is only now recovering.[NEW 21]

Chan Thomas had access and clearance and he was the first to mention galactic magnetism as the cause of the unlocking of the crust from the mantle.[NEW 28] He was also kept from successfully alerting the American public, and his 1960's book, *The Adam and Eve Story*, did not sell very well. He tried to bring his research to the awareness of America, but the power of the CIA was showing its broad reach. Now Chan Thomas' research has launched a new catastrophism with the input of Hannes Altven, who showed how external magnetic fields could overcome the inertial momentum of a rotating object that is magnetized and conductive—our Earth.[NEW 20-21] Chan Thomas suggested that a null point field at the galactic equator could disrupt Earth's polarity causing a polar reversal as our solar system crossed the plasma boundary of what we now call the Galactic Current Sheet. The Galactic Current Sheet spreads throughout the galaxy like ripples from a stone thrown into a pond. It's a double layer of tribo-electricity; one sheet positively charged, the other negatively charged. Cosmic dust is attracted (and repelled) along these waves, much as a Swiffer duster grabs dust and dirt.

Chan Thomas provided clues to point modern researchers in the right direction.[NEW 28] With subversive actions, the CIA controlled mainstream geological science using Hapgood as their dummy to sabotage any inquiry into catastrophism. Doug Vogt traced the funneling of funding through a tangled monstrosity of NSF grants, that revealed how the CIA was able to control a large portion of scientific publishing. The US government, the gatekeepers at key science journals and Ivy League science departments, starting with Columbia (as exposed by the Harvard Crimson in 1980)[NEW 22] have not been helpful in keeping us safe and prepared. Professors have lost grants, positions, and respect over this subject.[NEW 24] We'll need to do that on our own, unless we see sweeping changes.

Chan Thomas shifted the focus of scientists to galactic magnetism, providing enough clues to point research in the right direction. Doug Vogt's research on the isotopes, myths, extinctions, and climate records with Robert Felix's research on magnetic excursions, ice ages, and the extinctions and arise of new species, and evidence supporting theories of rapid glaciation/deglaciation by numerous scientists such as Randall Carlson, and the modern contributions of some of the same scientific journals that stymied the research a few years previous.[NEW 28-29]

What is changing is the North Magnetic Pole which has been meandering in Arctic Canada for years at about 5½ kilometers/year. It suddenly took off toward the Geographic North Pole at the breakneck speed of about 5½ kilometers/month. It raced across the Arctic Ocean toward Siberia, heading South toward a location research suggests will be the next North Polar ice cap in the Bay of Bengal between India and Indonesia; much too frigid for any but polar bears and seals, but they'll have to find their own way to get there. It's not likely any boats or ships will survive the event, either. The South Magnetic Pole has left Antarctica, headed north, but the next South Pole will most likely be offshore Peru and Ecuador. Not only are the Magnetic Poles in transit to elsewhere, but the whole magnetosphere of Earth is waking up, influenced by the magnetosphere of the Sun that has been activated as it moves through the Galactic Current Sheet of the Milky Way Galaxy. That also is the galactic magnetosphere that connects with the Plasma/Electric Universe. Plasma, a fourth state of matter, is atoms which, through electric stimulation and/or high heat has lost one or more electrons in its outer shell structure, producing its own unique light signature.

Most matter in the universe is cold plasma. We just can't see it because it's not in the process of losing electrons. It all connects—Earth to solar system to Galaxy to Interstellar space and the rest of the universe. Some species of whales that migrate, navigating by Earth magnetism, have errantly beached themselves.[68,70] Migrating birds have also been confused by these changes.

In 1958, the intelligence community organized the International Geophysical Year to gather information about the Earth that would shed light on this growing dilemma. They had made sure to establish the National Science Foundation in 1950 to fund the science they needed to foster. Then they needed to find out if the sun ever spewed out evidence of a nova. They initiated the Apollo program in 1967 to get samples from the lunar surface. Yes, the characteristic small glass spherules found on Earth in rock and alluvium layers deposited 12,000 years apart would be found all over the Moon. The analysis showed transuranic elements that are only created on the sun. To triple-check that, the US government created a Mars program to search for the same on Mars—it was there, too![GDJ 269-270]

Those programs came and went. They got what they needed—confirmation of a recurring micronova of our sun every 12,000 years. It never happened before in recorded history except at the time of the construction of Göbekli Tepe in Turkey at the end of the last Ice Age. The science of recurrent micronovas is new—but not to the CIA. They've known about this cataclysm ever since they sent Major White to the Arctic nearly a century ago, and **a cyclical crustal shift with recurring polar positions throughout geologic time has never been debunked.**[NEW 23]

I discovered a YouTube series by Doug Vogt that Penny Kelly had mentioned, and I watched him present what he learned until my three book purchases were delivered. I recognized that Mr. Vogt had possibly found the Rosetta Stone that had eluded Velikovsky. Creating a database of distances from Earth to stars, Vogt noticed regions in which no stars are seen. He wondered why the bands were empty and why these bands were 12,068 light years apart. He realized the stars **were** there but hidden behind dust. He eventually discovered that our Sun goes nova every 12,068 years.[GDI 41] Apparently, it's not the extreme cataclysm that destroys other stars, just coughing off dust and debris accumulated over 12,068 years, enough to cause Ice Ages, planetary floods, earthquakes, and volcanic eruptions. The sun stops in the sky and rises thereafter on a different horizon—the very phenomena that people around the planet described in their myths and stories, art, and song, just as Velikovsky had written half a century earlier.

The Electric Universe/Plasma Cosmology community have supported Velikovsky, showing the presence of high energy electromagnetic plasmas throughout the cosmos. They have also suggested that the sun is fed by intergalactic plasma currents, which may have their own periodicity, and which might support the idea of recurring micronovas. Mainstream astronomy is beginning to accept that the planets may not always have held their current positions, and that plasma is a powerful cosmological force—two of Velikovsky's key hypotheses.

Ages in Chaos, *Worlds in Collision*, and *Earth in Upheaval* were reported as ancient memories of cosmic catastrophes that people endured, and remembered. As a psychoanalyst, Velikovsky had learned that highly emotional events could live on in the collective unconscious as stories, myths, legends, and art, but his psychoanalysis was not widely accepted. On one of his YouTube videos, Vogt relates,"there are people who do not want wide social awareness about regular near-extinction events". That's why the US Government established, as cover operations, the International Geophysical Year, created the National Science Foundation, and the Apollo Space Program. They created it to send the young sun-gods to study the moon, cancelled it when they found the debris of a micronova on the lunar surface, and then sent a Mars rover on a mission to take soil samples on Mars, just to be sure. Same result. Our sun has a habit of cleansing itself of accumulated dust and debris, every 12,068 years.[GDJ 398]

Then I noted the mention of layers of black that another scientist had described as indicative of a comet striking the Earth. (I described this in my 1st book, *Dancing a Quantum Dream*). He mentioned the time at about 12,000 years ago. Vogt also described this layer connected to the recurring micronova of our Sun. Perhaps the comet theory was too limited. Perhaps the comet was part of a larger cataclysm nearly 12,068 years ago? It's all coming together. The North magnetic pole has moved into Siberia. We've been monitoring its movements for over a hundred years, but only geological evidence of shift to the opposite polarity. That might affect rotation and protection from gamma and cosmic rays by the magnetosphere. A micronova might erupt within the following decade or two... or three.

It has no connection to climate change except the increase in solar activity. It's why the global warming hysteria is another cover-up.[GDJ 285] If the North Magnetic Pole continues to move south, it is evidence of the prelude to a magnetic recursion being engineered by a change in the magnetosphere of the Sun prior to the micronova. It's just the first catastrophe in the cascade of catastrophes that might follow—instant Ice Age due to a fireball (CME) that blows away part of the atmosphere, sets fire to all that is not already under water, a magnetic fury that kills all electronics and transmission of electricity, initiates the eruption of earthquakes and volcanoes, the burning of cities, forests, grasslands and farms. Randall Carlson suggested "a solar super flare outburst will end that brief Ice Age as rapidly as it begins." Drs. Schoch and Peratt concur.[NEW 73]

Do you remember the color of the sun in past years? Yellow—now it's nearly white because of a change in solar activity. The awakening of our magnetosphere might affect rotation and protection from gamma and cosmic rays. A micronova could erupt within the following decade or two. The pattern change rate suggests the climax will be approximately in 2037-2047. Ben Davidson estimates that at the current rate of magnetic field loss, global grids will have serious problems by 2030-2040, and the best estimate for the magnetic recursion 2040-2060.[NEW 84]

We are entering the Galactic Current Sheet now[NEW 79] and it will take 20-30 years for the micronova to develop to the trigger point. Doug Vogt has predicted that the recurring micronova will happen around 2046.[GDJ 300] A bit of global warming would be dolls and teacups, by comparison. If you see your compass point the wrong way, the poles are moving. If the sun turns red, the next event is a black sun and that means you have only about 16 hours to get to your cave, or mine, for shelter from the impact of the shell that was covering the Sun. Wear and cover up as much as you can because the cosmic rays and X-rays can kill you. It will become like a civilization between stone age and bronze age —pre-agricultural if not pre-industrial. Camping will likely be a permanent lifestyle for quite a while.

Cellphones and iPads will no longer be of much use. Time to learn the secrets of the shaman. Gnostic higher consciousness and cardio-contemplation will have much value. My goal is to provide you with preparation for the oncoming **train** so you can survive and be a teacher for others who were not ready on time.

Siberian leaders sent their people on migrations south, east, and west. They stayed in their land to pass into the afterlife where they knew they would be conscious in a world of no time and no dimensionality. I've designed a do-it-yourself workshop to help you prepare for what is coming. To succeed you can use these tools to develop your deep understanding of the knowledge that leads to deep consciousness. Shaman comes from the Tungus language of Asia in which šaman means **one who knows**.[SFB 5]

The Greek for **knowing** is gnosis. I've found that many of the shamanic tools are also Gnostic.[IJ 5] They are almost interchangeable, but from different traditions. Those of us who do not survive the cataclysm will be in a world not ruled by time (eternity), and without dimension (infinity). This knowledge is my gift to you and the future of humanity. Death is not the end of existence, just the end of the experience of the world of time and space.

This book is intended to show you a way to respond to this harsh news in a way that can lighten the load as it brings light to heart and soul. Each chapter was designed to lead you through shamanic and gnostic channels of knowledge and wisdom. It's a deep course of preparation. Humans have survived many such cosmic catastrophes in the past, or we wouldn't be here to have this conversation. I am pouring into this book how you can succeed to carry on civilization anew, soundly grounded in the wisdom of the ages as well as deeply scientific revelations about what happens if you do not make it through the coming event.

This is a call to spiritually awaken to the expression of love that we truly all are, and to stand strong and deliver with our beautiful, amazing planet and all our cosmic kin. This is the time to get close to God and be more conscious of how we treat others. All we can do is love family and friends as much as possible, take nothing for granted and give as much as possible, because all of this can end at any moment. It's our time to be fully present and to go beyond the expectations we've had of ourselves as humans.

The good news is, of the geomagnetic excursions in the past 100,000 years or so, we have not experienced two bad ones in a row and the most recent one, 8/10, was bad. 10 of 10 would be extermination of all life on Earth.[NEW 33]

We have good reason to hope this coming event will be much gentler. 72,000 years ago in the Toba event, just a few dozen reproductive females survived, according to human genome research. But humans have survived. So, we can take heart that it is more than possible—it is in our genes. We are in charge of how we handle the emotional, mental shock of the event. Shock is perhaps our worst enemy and we are in charge of that.

Things might get scary but informed awareness will always trump fear, or ignoring what's coming. Meditation alone might not be enough to change your success, but deer-in-the-headlights is a way to fail. Training your brain to click into gear when needed is a vital part of prepping.

I'm giving you the information that can help you prepare mentally and spiritually, as well as deciding how to prepare so that you have a decent chance of surviving.

Mental practice is an active consciousness considering what you will experience, what you need to do to meet the challenge, and the tools or supplies you will need to be successful. To be forewarned is to be forearmed. Part of that armament is to get spiritually centered. That's next. That's the solid foundation for which we were designed, and a source from which you can draw, on the Grandmothers and the Grandfathers, as I have and as my Ojibwe ancestors did. I am with you all the way. I am White Eagle Soaring.

The spirals danced and swirled.
"That was like spiritual archaeology, digging up ancient memories," sang a Grandmother, shaking off stardust.
"Yeh" grinned a Grandfather. "Stardust wasn't the only debris. 80 years of a busy life is quite a load to sift through!"
"He had almost forgotten that strange recognition by that Viennese woman who had seen him holding the Earth together in that ayahuasca ceremony we had arranged so many Earth-years ago," intoned the Dreamkeeper.
"With his memory of his friend Jim, telling him that he had decided to sell DIRT GLUE… that was a great safety seal using humor to help him remember."
"He chuckled often to keep the message fresh in his mind. With his humor and awareness of synchronicity, he eventually discovered the message we gave him in Vienna."
"And who was that clown spirit who made up that company slogan—We Hold The Earth Together? THAT was brilliant!" whooped the DreamKeeper.
"That was me!" giggled a fairy-like angel and the Heavenly Host erupted in laughter and song.

Quantum Heaven, A Window To Consciousness

Because of the success of science in reviving dead or dying patients, near-death experiences began to happen amazingly often, and many people were able to share their experiences in the world of the afterlife in exquisite and coherent detail. Not just dozens, not hundreds, but thousands, and perhaps millions, many of them highly qualified medical doctors and scientists. Their stories have been corroborated again and again, and the evidence is spectacular: The evidence shows that there is consciousness **after** the brain dies.

Mellen-Thomas Benedict reported, "Since my return [from my near-death experience] I've experienced the light spontaneously, and I've learned how to get to that space almost any time in my meditation. Each one of you can do this. You don't have to die to do it. It is in your equipment; you are wired for it already." [POG 37]

"Be still and know that I am God."—Psalms 46:10

Evidence shows that consciousness is not a function of the brain but perhaps of non-resident Mind. Consciousness has to occur even before the brain exists. Neurosurgeon, Eben Alexander, M.D. was comatose for nearly a week and discussion had begun to bring his son back from college to attend his father's last moments.

"During my coma my brain wasn't working improperly —it wasn't working at all. I was encountering the reality of a world of consciousness that existed completely free of the limitations of my physical brain. My experience showed me that the death of the body and brain are not the end of consciousness, that human experience continues beyond the grave. The place I went was real. Real in a way that makes the life we're living here and now completely dreamlike by comparison. This life isn't meaningless. What happened to me while I was in that coma is hands-down the most important story I will ever tell. My conclusions are based on a medical analysis of my experience, and on my familiarity with the most advanced concepts in brain science and consciousness studies. Life does not end with the death of the body or the brain."—Eben Alexander, MD[POH 9-10]

Some of the most amazing evidence comes not from near-death experiences but from scientific inquiry, itself. From quantum physics, the latest paradigm of physics has superseded Newtonian physics, and is the source of our cellphones and transistors.

In quantum physics, objects are sometimes particles and sometimes waves, depending on an Intelligent Observer. That could be you or me or the postman, no difference. Humans are one with consciousness, without which the universe cannot exist—the lights would go out throughout the universe. Without Intelligent Observers—us—the cosmic movie, the light-show illusion of matter, will not play. Without Intelligent Observers, there can be no world, no universe. Who we are are co-creators, whether we know it or not."[POG 138]

"There is no object in space-time without a conscious subject looking at it."—Amit Goswami, Quantum Physicist

"We are what we think, all that we are arises with our thoughts, with our thoughts we make the world."—Buddha

"We are gods with amnesia."—Joseph Selbie.

"Born of God, we are spirit and cannot be anything else. All is Mind—one Mind. We are that Mind, but asleep—yet awakening, and God is that Mind eternally aware."—Jan Price, Near-Death-Experiencer[POG 140]

The saints and sages, who are just as aware of their subtle divine nature as we are aware of our physical bodies, know that their energy body template and the thoughts that shape it have an independent transcendent reality; theirs is not belief, it is knowing. This has been known in Siberia in the Tunguskan word **saman** taught by the shaman and among the Greeks as Gnosis, taught by the Gnostics.[POG 140]

Our bodies are like space suits, costumes we must wear to play our parts in a universe that has a time dimension on a 3D+ time stage. Most of us are not aware that we have a double existence, simultaneously in this world and in the energy-verse. This world is our familiar world of time and space dimensions. Our consciousness is non-local, which means we are connected to All That Is. We are truly co-creators. We are infinite and eternal. That we are like God has been confirmed by experimental quantum physics and the confounding requirement for an Intelligent Observer. The matter-wave functions to manifest matter, without which nothing matters.

Earth Dream Theater

This is for those who have eyes to see,
for those who have ears to hear,
who faintly recall who they really are
and now would remember another world backstage.

You are more than you seem—
life is the Theater of Dream.
You wrote the part,
choreographed the dance,
selected the set and scene.

You were hung by your heels
and given a jolting swat.
You cried,
bewildered,
gasping for air,
searing your lungs,
stunned by the bright lights,
shocked by the chill of birth water
evaporating from your skin.

* * *

You could not remember who you had been.
You had agreed to not remember
the essence of who you are.
Stage sets gave you a sense of place
referencing here from far.

Undeniably true, of course,
if that is the only truth we share,
masked by the agreement to play
a part in the Earth-reality show,
scripted by the Inner Heart of You
before you walked onstage.

Crafted scene by scene
to pretend of linear sequence
we call Time,
without which the universe would seem unreal.

Yet there's no such place as far away,
no such time as then
not a place called Here or There,
or such a time as never.

For we live in the Always and the Now
of the great quantum Silence of God
in the warmth of the Heart of All.

aaheart+++

A Window To Consciousness

I can't believe I wrote that 30 years ago. How could I know what I would later discover and experience. It didn't come from my brain, but from a deep **knowing**, as though a sage stepped in for a cameo appearance.

"I often say we are conscious in spite of our brain, not because of it. It's not the increased activity in a brain region that leads to such phenomenal experiences. It's actually the brain turning off."—Eben Alexander, Neurosurgeon

We don't need to die to escape the neural circuitry of our brain. We can rewire the brain to allow us to bypass the firestorm-creating circuitry that keeps us pre-occupied with our sensory perception that presents the holograph of our physical world. We can rewire our brain to support more subtle perception, intuitive thinking and higher feeling. We can rewire our brain to support direct experience of our godlike potential.[POG 148] I don't remember any intention to rewire. I can remember resisting flawed attempts to narrow my range of operation. Was that it? Was that the clue I was ignoring since I discovered the approaching cataclysm?

That Viennese woman who saw me in an ayahuasca-induced vision leading a group holding the Earth together was a messenger? Most of my life I was led to fulfill that mission, helping others applying their consciousness as co-creators of the universe, averting a cataclysm, or at least healing a problem our Sun is facing so that humanity on Earth is not destroyed. Faced with a similar dilemma Penny Kelly wrote "... maybe their [hippies] presence was more practical, like having enough mass consciousness on the planet to be able to totally modify swelling suns, travelling dust clouds, and rampaging oceans using consciousness." Consciousness and Energy. Vol 4, p.185

"It was looking like the only option we had was to develop consciousness. Could we make a concerted effort to develop our relationships with these other forms of consciousness who shared the reality with us and in doing so, lessen the effects of the nova cycle?" Consciousness and Energy. Vol 4, p.193

"By developing consciousness, we may be able to alter reality." Consciousness and Energy. Vol 4, p.212

"If we are going to survive the suns nova cycle, the key piece we need right now is the ability to communicate with the elements." Consciousness and Energy. Vol 4, p.219

Saints, sages, scientists, and near-death experiencers have all testified to consciousness as the underlying foundation of reality, not only because of their personal experience, but also due to the discovery of the Intelligent-Observer paradox that has mystified top physicists of the 20th and 21st centuries. Our very adaptable brains can be rewired to support this transcendent awareness.

Our brains can support the physical stillness and inward absorption—practices that reside at the heart of science and religion—to rein in the runaway firing of neural circuits that becloud our consciousness, so we can naturally experience those realities we have hidden from ourselves. Saints, sages, scientists, and near-death experiencers have shown us that we are in a cosmic movie created for our benefit which we have been gifted the role of director to make changes as we go and grow in wisdom.[POG 25-31]

The purpose of this book is to shine some light on some pathways to the knowledge we need to perform our due diligence in serving as the conscious co-creators we were designed to be. Some of our indigenous people remember. I discovered one such man, Eagle Bear, drumming and singing in front of a Trader Joe's nearby. His people still remember. We all need to return to that awareness of our role in keeping our sun and solar system in balance. It might make the difference between extinction or survival.

> Oh, my Spirit wake in light.
> On wings of eagle, we take flight.
> Soar 'tween the Earth and Sun,
> Love and peace will make us one.
>
> Stars being born, we take flight,
> To find the daybreak of our night
> We travel far above what seems,
> To find the sources of our dreams.
>
> aaheart+++

Ancient prophecies of many primal people warn us of the Earth-Sun system cleansing itself in cataclysmic fashion as it has done before, unless humanity listens to their whispered song. Any prophecy, however, can be altered by a change in consciousness, or at least eased somewhat. It is human consciousness that must first change.

First, who we are is eternal, without end, Amen. Second, our consciousness makes the matter-waves materialize—we are co-creators of Creation. We are all One. Everything is interconnected by energy. The universe is a web of inseparable energy patterns. A great mysterious plan affects our evolution as a species. The mystery is what we are here to experience. Other dimensions await our discovery. As we alter our states of consciousness, we attune ourselves to the forces of nature and begin to channel them through divine guidance. The age we live in, and whatever our path, it is one we have freely chosen."[SD 72-3]

We are here to ease the Earth/Sun through its regular cleansing. With tools of our consciousness—singing, chanting, praying, drumming—humanity has been developing for thousands of years to be prepared for this cleansing. In the past, it wrought cataclysmic destruction by fire, snow, ice, flood, volcanoes, CMEs, and earthquakes that happen every 12,000 years. Prophecies of many ancient peoples have alerted us that Earth and our Sun will cleanse themselves with cataclysmic fury. Our species has survived, so we must learn to listen to their subtle voices. We have time to learn how to use our consciousness as we were designed, to alter the cataclysm, ourselves, or both through advanced shamanism/Gnosticism. They are nearly the same, these are practices of knowing.

We are made of the same materials and energies, ordered by the same forces of Nature, created by the same Creator, warmed by the same Sun. We receive all of what we are from this Creation. We return this gift to the Creation and its Creator to be in balance, and walk in beauty under the canopy of stars in the heavens, dancing with the clouds and in the rain. Not in weakness, but in strength. Not as serfs or vassals but with the strength and power of co-creators. We are manifestations of a Sacred vision.

I AM a child of God's Universe.

> I dance and sing and play.
> Asleep I learn of WHO I AM
> And laugh throughout the day.
> I AM the Song of Peace.
>
> God's Universe has brought me into being
> to be a Master of Play.
> When I dance, I move the Stars
> and Heal the Earth.
> When I sing, the Winds are my Song
> and the Seasons my Rhyme.
> When I Play the Universe opens
> new dimensions, new Realities.
> Cosmic Joy is WHO I AM.
>
> aaheart+++

This vital energy of life is so difficult to study because it behaves oddly; it seems to exist not just in one place at a time, but everywhere all the time. Its non-local nature seems so beyond what we have come to expect of other forms of energy. What makes life even more difficult for quantum physicists is that by just watching an experiment, their own energy influences the results."[THC 42]

Quantum physics suggests we are all a part of, and contributors to a subtle energy field that operates by the rule of timeless connection and not the mechanical limit of miles and walls—non-locally. Non-locality refers to an energy intelligence field of which all that is, ever will be, has ever been, is forever a part. If that seems more like a prayer than a normal statement of science, you are beginning to sense the collision of modern science with mysticism."[THC 43]

Pearsall writes, "While modern biomedicine grew from the Newtonian mechanical model of the body, Chinese medicine derived from a view of the body as an energy-driven ecosystem in which health depends on a proper balance of energy forces flowing throughout that system. Talking about and trying to measure life energy is not something modern Western medicine is comfortable with, but Chinese medicine, like almost every other older form of medicine, has always emphasized an energetic approach to understanding disease and healing." and "the oldest and longest tested energetic medicines of the world have no trouble seeing the heart as both stuff and energy (particles and waves) at the same time—quantum energy."[THC 29]

There is one reality, and if we wish to comprehend that reality we must use all forms of inquiry, the science of religion and the science of matter. Both sciences have a common purpose—to understand the same reality. That establishes an underlying unity of science and religion even though each uses different methods to explore the same reality. The two approaches use very different languages—math vs words, laws vs parables, theories vs allegories—all of which seem to describe very different realities. Because of these difficulties, there are very firmly held biases in each camp that spill over into the broader culture.[POG 1]

Oddly, it was philosophers who were the first scientists to try to understand and explain reality. Their explanations were adopted by the dominant religion of the time and it became church dogma. The promotion of the sun-centered astronomical observations of Copernicus, supported by Kepler's refinement of planets circling the sun in ellipses instead of circles around the Earth was not enough to permit acceptance of any mere theory that demoted the Earth from its place in the center of the universe. This was seen by the Church to be an insult to their god, a demotion of the primacy of God, and the primacy of the Church. The Inquisition could not allow such an affront.[QE 22-23]

Knowing what the Church would do to his brash insights, Copernicus withheld his new sun-centered model of the solar system until just before his death. Kepler held his refinement out of the controversy. Galileo didn't like being gagged, but shown the dungeons and torture devices, he kept silent. He realized if he were to do science, it could not be expressed as a contradiction to Church Doctrine, so he demolished Aristotle's explanations by the demonstrations of experiments.[QE 21-26] He knew the Earth moved, and Aristotle's explanation of motion would not happen on a moving Earth. Friction, not 'desire for rest at the cosmic center' is what made the feather fall more slowly than a rock. This is how he destroyed the powerful hypocrisy of the church and its threatening hold on functional advancement of science, which was successful in changing the way scientists thought and worked.

Galileo contrived situations to demonstrate that Aristotle's philosophy was wrong, He focused on only those questions that could be demonstrated, not just quibbled upon. He had created a science that demanded experimental demonstration as the only criterion for acceptance, and science progressed with the vigor of success. But it was a success based on narrowing the approach of science to an explanation of reality.[QE 25-27]

Classical Physics permits isolating consciousness and its free will from the world with which the Physicist should consider, dividing mind from matter, avoiding problems that deal with consciousness or free will. Therefore, science could avoid free will and consciousness and leave such matters to theology, philosophy, and psychology. That seemed like a clean break from such determinism, until quantum mechanics came along with a dilemma, or two. Max Planck had electrons behaving badly—randomly.[QE 33]

Then came a more profound challenge. Without an Intelligent Observer, matter waves would not show their other form of existence as particles. It was a paradox. For thousands of years philosophers had diverse views on the nature of reality. Realism considers the existence of the physical world to be independent of observation. It just is! Worse, realism might even insist anything not physical does not exist! This realism is called materialism, and is a prominent philosophy of science today.[POG 6-11]

In contrast to Newtonian materialism or realism, the philosophy of idealism says that what we perceive through our senses is NOT the actual world, although we can grasp the actual world with our mind. Taken to extremes of faithfulness to the philosophy, the solipsism of the puzzle of the tree falling in a forest can seem silly. But then, the same applies to materialism that posits that without physical forces impressed upon it, an object is not connected to the rest of the Universe. One could codify it as the **law of separability**. Einstein scoffed at this as **spooky actions**, but experiments show they happen.

Another way to view the world is by reductionism, by reducing a complex system to its simpler parts. Classic reductionism propose a simplistic explanation in lieu of a factual one. Not knowing what is causing an effect, biologists suggested the name **vital force** as a placeholder to explain effects they couldn't otherwise explain. Challenged to explain his force of gravity, Newton claimed that a theory should do no more than consistently provide correct predictions. His theory of gravity proclaimed a mysterious force transmitted through nothingness. Quantum Theory is an even more mysterious enigma.

A pebble dropped in a pond will show ripples spreading in a circular manner. When another stone is dropped in the pond near the first, crossing the ripples of the first stone, its ripples will add to the height making a deeper wave by making the trough between even deeper. The effect will create higher waves and deeper troughs. If a barrier with two slits is placed in the path of these two waves, the higher waves and deeper troughs passing through the slits will create an interference pattern. If light were a stream of particles, this interference pattern would not happen. Waves explain what we see. So, we had two competing theories to explain light, waves and particles called photons. Both could be proved but particles could not be understood as waves, nor waves as particles.[QE 62-63]

In 1923, American physicist Arthur Compton discovered that when light bounced off electrons, its frequency changed. That was not how light should behave if it were a wave! When Compton assumed that light was a stream of particles, each with the energy of Einstein's photon, there was a perfect fit to his data. It became known as the Compton effect. As a graduate student, the aristocratic Prince Louis de Broglie shared Einstein's sense that light has a dual reality. He proposed that perhaps matter was also either a particle or wave. His mathematical expression showed symmetry in Nature; what works to explain energy also explains matter, and the reverse. It's called the de Broglie wavelength and is central to a study of quantum mechanics. But we still don't know what in an electron vibrates! He had taken his idea to his thesis professor who was not impressed by de Broglie's suggestion, so he showed it to Albert Einstein, who was delighted.[QE 70-71]

In a minor accident in a telephone company laboratory in New York, Clinton Davisson proved that matter could be waves.[QE 71] The first hint of the quantum nature of reality, at first ignored, was finally forced upon physicists to admit that the physical reality of an object depends on how you choose to observe it. Consciousness is part of reality. Schrodinger's Cat broke the news that there was no magical theorist to resolve the wave-particle paradox. One hundred years later it still stands tall and defiant, as though to demand recognition, as if there were still doubt that Consciousness is in charge.

Ervin Schrodinger was a maverick. He rejected a physics where electrons were only allowed specific orbits, not permitted to give off radiation as was expected of everything else, and then give off radiation without any cause. All effects must have a cause or two! He saw de Broglie's matter waves as a way to get rid of Bohr's 'damn quantum jumps' by explaining them. He wanted an orderly world in which electrons and atoms behaved reasonably! His equation was received by Einstein with adulation, saying it was a work of genius. Werner Heisenberg, Bohr's young post doc countered with his own abstract expression of quantum mechanics. Schrodinger answered by showing Heisenberg's theory was logically congruent with his own, but by a different mathematical pathway.[QE 73-77]

Einstein had a deep conviction that the moon must exist even if he is not looking at it. He found it difficult to believe that God rolls dice, referring to the mathematics of equations usually expressed in terms of probability, so he searched for hidden properties, or any theory that could avoid the paradox of the need for an Intelligent Observer to make the matter-wave become matter.[POG 11]

Not only did no alternative theory show up, but several mathematical proofs ruled them out. Nils Bohr observed that Einstein should stop telling God what to do with His dice. Yet David Bohm discovered that hidden property in the cosmos—the universe is interpenetrated by a non-local realm—in which distance did not exist. Hard to imagine, but in 1964, John Stewart Bell presented a theorem that proved that not only could non-locality be a legitimate property of the real world, but the mathematics of quantum physics required it be so. Non-locality is now an accepted and non-negotiable feature of physics. Without it, quantum physics falls apart.[POG 75] Bohm received a Nobel Prize, made significant contributions to the Manhattan Project, and became a fellow of England's Royal Society.

But he was not satisfied. Finally, he realized the math showed the entire cosmos is one continuous, interconnected whole because nothing can be separate from anything else! Everything in the universe is invisibly connected to a pre-space 2-Dimensional realm in which undivided wholeness is in flowing motion.[POG 76-77] Einstein's hidden properties could not exist in our local 3D universe, but they could exist comfortably in non-local 2D pre-space. Bohm showed that the universe and everything within it emerges into being, conforming to a hidden order that exists in pre-space. He called it the Implicate Order.[POG 77-78] Fold an index card in half and you can get a physical model to hold in your hand to visualize this. When closed, it models the implicate universe; you're in a 2D pre-space. Open the card and you model the explicate universe of 3 Dimensions, the explicate order, our familiar realm in the cosmos.

Bohm went on to discover how a hologram works. A hologram is a 2D pattern like a photographic slide that, when placed in a projector, projects a 3D image.[POG 79] I'm reminded of a Viewmaster, a child's toy that used two images that when projected creates a 3D image. It's called The Holographic Principle. It's not an off-beat fringe theory—it became the basis for string theory and won the 1999 Nobel Prize for Leonard Suskind and Gerard 't Hooft, and inspired Juan Maldecena to publish a 1997 paper on string theory that by 2010, was cited 7,000+ times."[POG 80]

Just like a TV screen is made of tiny dots that light up to create an image, the universe is theoretically made up of billions of dots that create our hard reality. It is so dense you can't put your hand through it—solid. The order that Einstein sought has been identified, but it's non-local.[POG 81]

Bohm's mathematically sound interpretation of quantum physics, his implicate and explicate order, and string theory's use of his holographic principle, all support the testimony of the saints, sages and near-death experiencers. The heavens are the template for the universe which is being continuously created from a two-dimensional hologram in a pre-space, non-local D-brane, creating a three-dimensional holographic projection. The physical universe has no independent hard reality.[POG 83]

Meister Eckhart stated, "God is creating the entire universe, fully and totally, in this present now." Because we are conscious Intelligent Observers[POG 83] we are co-creators in this universe—no observers' license or diploma required. It's what we do naturally as the eternal WHO.

Jesus said, "There will be signs in the sun and moon and stars, and on the Earth anguish of nations not knowing the way out."—Luke 21:25

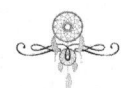

The spirals danced and swirled.
"Those are such happy words," sang a Grandmother.
"He has learned to listen very well!" smiled a Grandfather.
"He still has a few things to sort out, but he is making great progress putting it all together," rumbled the Dreamkeeper.
"It's almost a conversation now, he's become very receptive and responsive."

The Physics Of Co-Creation

Science has discovered in Quantum Theory that an Intelligent Observer must be watching photons of light or they will only be present as waves, and matter will not show up as particles. Consciousness must be present, or the Universe would not **matter**. Science has also shown that our consciousness does not originate in the brain. Consciousness is a feature of Creation, so we are co-creators of everything that **matters**. Who created all this? Creatures must be Created for it all to work. We are created before we were born and will continue to exist, even after our bodies die. Thousands of near-death experiences have told us about that. Creation cannot be created without a Creator and its co-creators. Max Tegmark at MIT suggested that consciousness might be a quantum state of matter.[POG3]

Scientific materialism has shown great success urging God toward retirement because we thought God was no longer needed to explain things like creation, life, and consciousness. But hidden in all that success was one nagging question: what is consciousness?

Scientists could find a scientific materialist explanation for life in complex organic chemistry, even for the development of life by complex theories of evolution. But consciousness has proven difficult to define, much less duplicate, in the confines of a scientific materialism. They haven't been able to find where in the body consciousness resides or originates—it's definitely not in the brain. In fact, with only deep meditation, two members of the Theosophical Society, Annie Bessant and Charles Leadbetter, were able to discover and describe quarks in the nucleus of an atom which were not known during their lifetimes, many years ahead of nuclear physicists.[POG XVII]

There is, and can only be, one reality. Bessant and Leadbetter used deep meditation (the science of religion) to study reality, whereas material scientists use rigorously controlled experiments and very technical tools (the language of mathematics). Spiritual scientists use rigorously controlled transcendent experience, an esoteric language of myth and allegory, to investigate the same reality. But neither seems able to work with the other group, as though each is a foreign culture. They are foreign belief systems, and the science of matter and energy considers its beliefs to be the only true religion. There is a deeply held belief that science is the only credible, true religion and no non-material viewpoint has any value. And yet, a 2009 poll by Pew found that only 41% of scientists considered themselves to be atheists, while 51% believed in God, a universal spirit, or a higher power.[POG 6]

Bessant and Leadbetter's amazing ability to see a subatomic level shows that humans are able to experience very unusual mastery, to intuit knowledge, to discover unexpected truths, perform real miracles that cannot be explained, do healing beyond knowing, attain unimagined states of peace, harmony, and love. There might be a similarity in language and practice, but I have found that there are some core practices that can be learned or taught, but even those can be learned intuitively if you simply allow silence, clearing of mind, and going into a deep inner stillness and listen. Sometimes, just listening to the quiet wisdom of the heart, you might be able to hear a soft voice of wisdom that speaks. Medicine men of my people call this the sissagwad, which is the soft whisper of the gentle spirit wind in the trees.

Even before I met the shaman, I had been following a child-like practice of listening to the sound of clouds in the sky. Even my quiet work on the tractor (work that required very little mind), I was able to essentially meditate, just be, and listen to the sissagwad. As a kid, growing up on a farm in Minnesota, I was letting life happen as I tuned into the heartbeat of the Earth, sun, and stars.

Come World

Come world,
mirror to me
who I Am.

I would know
that which is true,
the face behind the mask,
I think I see.

I see who I Am,
blood and bone and sinew—
substance moving among objects,
a thing among worlds,
ticking like a clock.

Pumps, tubes, levers.
I feel WHO I am—
warm, vibrating.
Pain opens me to my core
and I touch the real ME.

* * *

I hear who I am
marking time with my blood.

Yet in my dreams
I fly among the stars
and beyond,
and stand firmly rooted
in the silence of mountain
to look upon the land
and the surging sea.

I play among clouds,
always changing
and yet without form.

I AM more than I seem.
Who then am I
to stand the turning of the days?

Cloaked in other men's inspirations
fed me by the dead bones
that masquerade as learning—
unfold the child that hides
sacred in the heart
and whispers softly
in the wind of my soul.

Hear now, the soft and stormy musings
of the Body of All Being
that roars in Its Creation of the Elements
and blazes forth Its Fields of Possibility

across the limitless reach of my Imagination,
a Universe of Light
and being,
and I know WHO I AM

I Am a Child of God's Universe,
Through my eyes the Stars can see
the brightness of a billion suns
the Cosmos knows through me.

I am the Light of Peace
Twenty billion years of endless growth and change,
Particles becoming atoms drawn together in common Fire.
Kindling the furnace of all the stars
And blazing elements into existence.

Since the beginning, I am.
I Am a Child of God's Universe,
With my voice mountains speak.
The truth of Oneness stills my soul
And echoes from each peak.

I am the Voice of Peace.

Mountain stands patiently, silently.
She has been waiting for me to know and understand
The wisdom embedded in her rocks,
Roots gripped deep into God's Earth,
And I know WHO I AM.

I Am a Child of God's Universe,
When I listen, Oceans hear—

The gliding sea bird's call of life,
A robin's call of cheer.

I am the Sound of Peace.

Four billion years of endless growth and change,
Through countless forms tried and tested,
A playful Creator brought me out of the sea,
To know Its beauty in my special way,
To love All of WHO I AM.

I Am a Child of God's Universe,
With my fingers clouds can touch
The loving softness of the Earth
That nurtures All of Us.

I touch the Heart of Peace.

Three million years of endless growth and change,
Of knowing, forgetting, and learning again
To touch the Earth with gentleness
And reverence that honors the fullness,
The Mystery of Who I AM.

aaheart+++

What Is Consciousness?

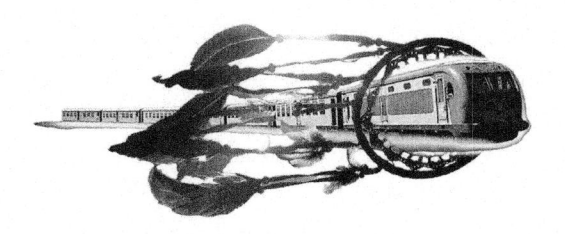

Hours of walking in the woods, gathering and eating gooseberries, driving one of our tractors and feeling the warmth of the sun on my skin, becoming one with the sun, clouds, and stars was my early, natural preparation to be a shaman and Gnostic.

As an adult, I attended a meditation at a friend's house in celebration of what they called the 11:11 convergence. We began with a meditation. All I knew about meditation was to be quiet and *go inside and listen*. So, I did.

After a few minutes we were to awaken. So, I did.

We were asked to share our experience of our meditation. So I did.

I told them that all I had seen was blackness, but there was a strange brilliance to that blackness. Decades later, I discovered that one of the experiences of Gnostic initiates as they developed their awareness of God was what they called the experience of *dazzling darkness*. This was the experience of being in the presence of God as though you were sitting in his lap as his light shone past you and lit up the darkness around you. So, the darkness around you dazzled with the Light of God. That's what I experienced that night so many years ago! I had no idea! That's why the poetry I write seems to come to me so naturally and has such an otherworldly feel to it! I'm a Gnostic and didn't know it! Somehow, I had fallen into a way of being that is shamanic and gnostic.

I share this with you because you need to know that this can be available to you, too. I also learned to be playful and always open to wonder and curiosity. Even when I was in my middle years, my friend Deanie would call to tell me about a new adventure she wanted to share, and I would drive over to her apartment and play with ideas. One time she had an idea about a way to arouse someone from gloomy self-deprecation with a huge spike painted gold to offer them when they were in self-crucifixion mood. That's how I created a children's book to encourage them to identify with nature by collecting Grandfather Story Stones and listen to their stories, or use clear marbles to teach the value of the present moment that is a few chapters further on in this book.

Another time she called to ask if I knew how to weave dreamcatchers, and since I had puzzled that out in my head at a powwow a week earlier, said, "I think so." She started me on a career as a teacher of dreamcatcher weaving, selling my dream catchers in workshops across the country and around the world on my own website that I brought into the top 20 on Google.

<blockquote>
I Am a Child of God's Universe,
Through my joy Earth celebrates
The passion of Creation—
The Smile upon my face.

I Am the Face of Peace.

Through eons of endless forms and change
God's universe has Created many expressions of joy
</blockquote>

> And playful intelligences that have echoed
> Cosmic Wit and Grace beyond Time and Space,
> The essence of Who I AM.
>
> I Am a Child of God's Universe,
> With my Heart Creation Loves,
> Reflecting all the peace and joy
> that lives in all of us.
>
> I AM the Heart of Peace.
>
> aaheart+++

We live in an illusion. We think it is 'hard reality' but it's mostly empty space around us. Matter is not what it seems. Many religious traditions are okay with that. Hinduism, Buddhism, Jainism, and Sikhism understand that we see, hear, and feel through a veil of illusion. Science has proved this to be true. Our eyes only see a limited range of wavelengths of light, but not beyond red at one end of the spectrum, or purple and indigo at the other. Other wavelengths of light are there but our eyes are not able to see them. Most of what is there, we can't see. Thousands of other colors are invisible to us, but we can see just the seven colors of the rainbow, and the transitional colors between. Our ears can hear sounds in a similarly limited range—from 20-20,000 Hz. Some bats can hear sounds up to 200,000 Hz. Atoms can vibrate at 10,000,000,000,000 Hz. At the low end, earthquakes, volcanoes, and lightning create very low frequencies in the range of 0.001 Hz—the world is bustling with sound. Smell, taste, and touch are also severely limited. Matter is a circus of vibrating energy.[POG 40]

Yet, an atom is mostly nothing. That silly diagram of the simplest atom—Hydrogen—though useful in teaching, is off by an enormously misleading scale. We've known for more than a century that if that model were to be drawn to scale, the electron would have to be circling several miles away. If we were to remove all the empty space in the matter that makes up our bodies, we would be so tiny we could dance on a pinhead."[POG 41]

So, if we get slammed against a wall, why don't we go through it? The model doesn't show the electron moving... at about 1,800 miles/second! Our atoms are more than screaming around the track! The electrons create an impenetrable cloud, a force field around every atomic nucleus—that makes it hard!"[POG 42]

Finally, the third problem with that diagram is that the dot in the middle of the atom that's supposed to represent the nucleus, isn't solid either. It's a force field, too. Protons and neutrons are also whizzing around an even smaller track. Einstein showed that with his famous E=MC² and proved it with atom-smasher experiments. He showed there are many other parts to a nucleus of an atom—quarks, bosons, hadrons, fermions, photons, gluons, mesons, baryons, leptons, muons, pions, kaons… nope, no Klingons, that's Star Trek! Then they discovered the Higgs's field, which in theory gives matter its mass (resistance to being in motion)—energy interacting with another energy."[QE 45]

Everything is energy. Everything our senses can sense is energy. Even matter is a light-show illusion, an invisible organization of energy, but it's there, just not what it seems. Matter isn't fixed, not a permanently unchanging something."[POG 48]

As huge as this universe is, it's the smaller something of the everything. For decades, physicists have guessed that there must be another part of the universe that is only two dimensional, made of pure energy that is even bigger than this universe. Perhaps we could call it Heaven, as saints and sages have called it."[POG 49]

Our three-dimensional universe is sort of a bubble in a practically infinite two-dimensional ocean of energy that could be called an energyverse. Saints and sages have known this through their own transcendent experience. Physicists were finally forced to conclude that the amount of matter and energy cannot quite explain what happens and shows up. Einstein's equations suggested that the universe should be contracting rapidly. In fact, it should never have expanded as much as it has—or even formed at all.[POG 52] Something was missing for scientists.

Surprisingly, Hubble discovered that the expansion of the universe is *accelerating*. This led to an amazing discovery that all the detectable matter accounts for only 4.9% of the gravity. They imagined dark matter and dark energy to fill the void, and still came up short. So, they posited a new way to account for the energy using String Theory, which suggests a part of the universe that we can't see interpenetrates everything. It's filled with teeny vibrating rings and strings of pure energy that vibrates at wavelengths too small to be detected by our measuring instruments. The small amount of detectable matter is almost a tiny by-product. According to String Theory, the energyverse is so vast it has room for many millions of three-dimensional energy bubble universes like ours.[POG 54] Jesus said, "In my father's house there are many mansions." Prescience?

Using the equations of Relativity theory, physicists calculated there should be 10-9 joules/cubic meters of space. But using the equations of quantum theory the energy should be 10-113 joules of energy/cubic meters of space. That's a magnitude of 122X! That missing energy must be somewhere[POG 56-57] so the physicists came up with M-Theory, a version of string theory that must exist some other place than in the four dimensions of space and time beyond which our senses and our instruments are unable to detect.

In M-Theory, all dimensions exist in 'branes', a contraction of the word 'membrane', suggesting a barrier or boundary that separates one region from another. M-Theory posits that there are rather small branes that enclose any three-dimensional branes from super-large branes that are two-dimensional. Combined, all branes make up the cosmos, some of which is visible and accessible to us.

In M-Theory there is a specialized class of branes called D-branes which are three-dimensional, but opaque and inaccessible. M-theorists say we are stuck in our D-brane, unable to go to other branes or even detect them.[POG 57] Our three-dimensional, energy bubble, D-brane universe is a light-show illusion, created and sustained by an underlying, invisible two-dimensional energyverse.

We not only exist in a 3-dimensional bubble, a physical universe, we also depend upon a 2-dimensional energyverse that is continuous, and inter-penetrating our physical universe at every point. This makes the physical universe one with the energyverse. Each of us inhabit both realms, which makes the material body inseparable from our energy body. Like our universe, our bodies are an ultra-high-definition holographic projection, continuously created according to our personal holographic energy template.[POG 81-85]

Saints, sages, and near-death experiences inform us that we each have our own personal holographic energy template, our energy body, from which the high-res holographic projection of our physical body originates, and moment by moment it determines everything about our physical body. The saints and sages variously call this the astral body, subtle body, etheric body, or spirit body, vibrating at frequencies impossible to measure. Our physical body has lower frequency energies that can be detected. This low energy-frequency is held in organized patterns by the higher-frequency energy body. Experiential religious traditions of the world—yoga, T'ai Chi, Sufism, charismatic Christianity, and cardio-contemplation might call these subtle energies, Life Force.

Working with this force is the core of many commonly accepted healing practices, from Chiropractic to Acupuncture. Individuals who use these practices are often called intuitives or clairvoyants. They can see or sense the energy body as a multi-colored aura, or halo.[POG 86-88]

Learning to deeply perceive and control the subtle energy body is the first step on the journey to finding the stillness and inner absorption essential to transcending experience, as the energy body becomes sacred. In Christianity, it's sometimes called *Holy Ghost* or *Holy Spirit* as gateways to divine experience. As a kid, I didn't try to describe it. I just did it. Even though I was to have lights out by 9pm, I used a flashlight and pulled the bedcovers over my head to read the King James Version, cover to cover, long past my bedtime. Author James Selbie writes: "Today, by using meditation and pranayama, I can experience that surpassing state of awareness—which I discovered accidentally through drugs—but now through much more reliable, consistent, and lasting means."[POG 89]

Alas, string theory's vast conceptions of a multidimensional universe has not had much impact on biology and genetics. Professionals who try to use this new paradigm get a chilly reception, such is the firm grip of scientific materialism and the effectiveness of its own form of inquisition and prejudice.

The odds against the universe existing are so astronomically heart-stopping that the notion it merely happened defies common sense. It would be like tossing 10 quintillion coins and they all come up heads.

Quantum physicists ran into some unexpected weirdness early on that lead to amazing discoveries:

The Uncertainty Principle—Physicists can't measure all properties of atom-sized objects at the same time. You could not know both position and momentum at the same moment. This was called the Heisenberg uncertainty principle. That's like your GPS and speedometer would not work at the same time.

Wave-Particle Duality—Energy, light, and atoms can behave like a wave or a particle.[POG 70]

The Intelligent Observer Paradox—resolving Wave-Particle Duality and the Heisenberg uncertainty principle was complicated because matter-waves behave like matter only when measured by an Intelligent Observer.[POG 71]

These weirdness problems were partially resolved by choosing to ignore them. This was called the Copenhagen interpretation. That leaves a lot of questions on the table. Another quantum weirdness problem was the question of when two matched particles split in an atom smasher, a change in the spin of one resulted in an immediate matching change in the spin of the other, even though the particles were each traveling apart faster than the speed of light, exceeding the speed limit for light as Einstein's Theory of Relativity had established. That would be impossible! Einstein was sure of that! That would prove that there was a significant flaw in the theory. In a short time Quantum Physicists did the experiment and the impossible was shown to have happened! They developed a new theory that supposed that the particles existed in a two-dimensional brane in which the particles that existed weren't that far apart, so they didn't have that missing dimension to travel. This weirdness confirmed the existence of a 2D brane.[POG 73-74]

Quantum physicists were also confused when it was discovered that an Intelligent Observer was necessary for matter to happen. Matter can exist as a wave or particle, but it can only show up as a solid expression of the wave if an Intelligent Observer is doing the measuring. To simplify the problem: our consciousness is a vital function in the formation of matter! [POG 78]

Quantum physicist, Amit Goswami makes it quite clear, "There is no object in space-time without a conscious subject looking at it." And you don't need a degree from MIT to do it!

If matter has no predetermined permanent form until a conscious being observes it, science can no longer claim that material objects exist independent of consciousness. Their religion of materialism collapses under this crushing discovery. A century ago, they found a mathematical work-around, quantum mechanics, to allow them a way to get on with their work, without solving the ultimate mystery of reality. It remains unsolved today. Physicist Nick Herbert at Berkeley summed up their dilemma with a wry grin, saying, "One of the best kept secrets of science is that scientists have lost their grip on reality." [POG 12]

Not only have we seen that classical Newtonian physics cannot explain everything, even the most modern physics of quantum mechanics cannot explain this because most physicists are hobbled by the limitations of their materialist religion. Saints, sages, and near-death experiences might be able to show the way.

The need for an intelligent, conscious observer is not the only gaping hole in this scientific materialism. In 50 studies of physiological changes (when a person with multiple personalities changes from one personality to another), it was discovered that although one personality was allergic to specific allergens, other personalities in that individual were not. One personality might be left-handed while other personalities in that same body were right-handed. One personality might need glasses, whereas other personalities in the same body did not. In a study on eyesight in which many characteristics were recorded for each of 10 personalities in one person, the eyes changed with each personality, including the color of the iris.[POG 12-13] That's genetically impossible.

Until 1995, the CIA, in their Stargate program had studied remote viewing in 22 labs around the United States. The program was abandoned because the information was not consistently valid—but it was valid. The final report stated that a "statistically significant effect has been observed." It just wasn't close enough to 100% to make it reliable but far beyond mere chance.[POG 14]

Sara Paddison, at the Institute of HeartMath, has written that their research found a heart-to-heart connection that operates in a higher frequency band than the mind. Paul Pearsall notes that she may be referring to what he has called *L-energy*, the mind to which she refers is the *heartless brain*, of a brain/heart/body Mind of cardio-energetics, a heart-to-heart connection, a unique power when two hearts connect. Dr. Pearsall explains, "By silencing your brain and freeing yourself from its constant, annoying urging you to do or think something, by being still enough in the presence of other hearts to allow your heart to be receptive and open to the energy coming to it. By allowing yourself to experience the subtle L-energy connection to your own heart, and yet being aware of the energy going out from your heart to other hearts, your heart becomes no longer just yours, but ours."[THC 171-3] This might be a form of praying together and the way the created become one with the Creator.[THC 166]

"For where two or three are gathered together in my name, there am I in the midst of them."—Matthew 18:20

"Silence is the language God speaks."—Thomas Keating, Trappist Monk

David Bohm, a pioneer in the study of quantum physics, wrote *Wholeness and the Implicate Order* in which he explained that all reality is inseparably interconnected, proving mathematically that no object can exist separately from any other. John von Neumann, considered one of the greatest mathematicians of the 20th century, asserted that consciousness doesn't just affect reality, consciousness creates reality. In his book, *The Nature of the Physical World*, astrophysicist, Sir Arthur Eddington wrote, "The stuff of the world is mindstuff... no one can deny that mind is the first and most direct thing in our experience and all else is inference."[POG 14-17]

Fritjof Capra (*The Tao of Physics*) and Amit Goswami (*The Self-Aware Universe*) both professors of physics and authors, exhibit some of the thinking of a new generation of physicists familiar with Eastern spiritual philosophies: "An increasing number of scientists are aware that mystical thought provides a consistent and relevant philosophical background to the theories of contemporary science, a conception of the world in which the scientific discoveries of men and women can be in perfect harmony with their spiritual aims and religious beliefs."—Fritjof Capra

"Instead of positing everything (including consciousness) is made of matter, this philosophy posits that everything (including matter) exists in and is manipulated from consciousness."—Amit Goswami

The material bias of science that leads many nonscientists to decide that many beliefs underlying religion have been disproven—is an unfounded bias. A minority of scientists believe solely in the religion of scientific materialism, whereas not one of religion's core beliefs—miracles, life after death, heaven, God, or transcendent experience—has been ruled out by science. A widespread acceptance of scientific materialism's unproven beliefs gives that illusion.[POG 17] The science of religion is a collection of disciplines, usable by anyone, which, when performed with determined focus and intention, inevitably result in personal transcendent experience.

If a farm kid growing up in Minnesota can stumble into a lifetime of transcendental experiences as I have, you can, with more focus and purpose, surpass what I have done. I had a lot of help and that help is available at no cost to you. Just call on the Grandmothers and Grandfathers for help. There's a lot more of them than there are of us. They are expert, tireless, and persistent. And they love doing it. Just be silent and listen exquisitely.

I was driving from Denver to Santa Monica for a Native American Art show when I began to feel a bit sick. I struggled through the Art Show and after it was over, I decided to forego my planned marketing and head back to Denver to recover. I used a healing trick I learned from my dad to put on sweaters, cover with lots of blankets to sweat it out. When I awakened the next morning, a voice was calling my name gently. After looking to see who was calling me, the voice asked me if I would dance a new dream for the people that they might live. I said yes, and then asked what that meant. The answer was that *they* would be showing me. I thought the answer I got was that I would market my dreamcatchers in Europe where I was told that that was where the pebble of ego had been dropped into the pond of consciousness. So, when I had done that, I thought I had accomplished my commission.

But what I didn't know was that a train was on the tracks, and it was getting closer. When I finished writing *Dancing a Quantum Dream* I realized that I had been led to discover that the Train on the Track was nearly here so I began more deeply examining my life experiences and with guidance from the Grandmothers and Grandfathers discovered the recurrent micronova that wasn't even in the news This book is the fulfillment of that commission except that I still have time to spread the word.

The spirals danced and swirled.
"He has awakened! He knows!" a grandmother gasped. "He has become one who knows!"
"To become one who knows, he has had to choose the hidden path and live an open life," smiled a Grandfather. "His openness to the spirit was what he chose while still a child!"
"This was his choice even before he was born," nodded the Dreamkeeper. "That was why he wanted to come back, to dance the new dream for his people that they might live with a happy and free spirit."
"When he spoke to the people at the powwow his voice carried power," cooed a grandmother. "And his feet scarcely touched the ground when he danced!"
"He was allowing my voice to come through him," winked the Dreamkeeper. "Even the chief was amazed and asked if he would speak for him one day."
"And not worried about so many people watching, he healed Grandfather Oak with his hands and a rattle, before the whole powwow," a Grandmother purred.
The spirals whirled and danced in grace and beauty.

Smudging And The Sage Ceremony

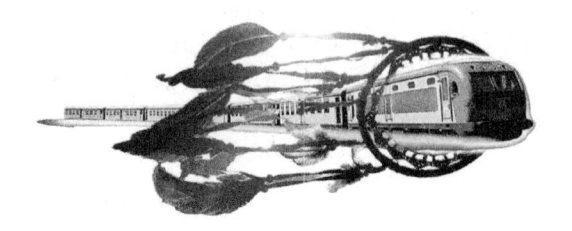

At the heart of shamanic practice, the Shaman makes an intimate connection to the spirit world by honoring the natural beings around him and calls upon them to assist in interacting with the world of natural spirits for many purposes, notably healing. This is a deep honoring of the world in which we live, building a greater awareness of our intimate connections so readily pushed aside by modern technological civilizations who in many ways, has lost its sense of connection to the natural world.

Smudging has been used since ancient times by many people as a ceremony of cleansing and purification among pre-Christian pagans as well as Catholic and Eastern Orthodox churches, among Hindus and Buddhists as well as Cherokee, Ojibway, and Lakota. Called 'incense' in some traditions, it can be made of a variety of fragrant plant materials. Native American have used their local plants or obtained more exotic plant materials through trade with the tribes of other regions. Among the plants they used for smudge are tobacco, sweetgrass, calamus, red willow bark, red osier dogwood bark, cedar needles, and sage. (This is not the culinary sage of the genus, Salvia. Rather it is one of the species, Artemisia Tridentata, which includes the landscape perennials, Silver King and Silver Mound, as well as sagebrush.)

I have gathered sage in many parts of the U.S., from Minnesota to the Rocky Mountains of Utah, California, Oregon, and Washington State. The plant material you choose should be partially dried in the open under sunny skies, so it does not mold as it finishes drying. It is best ready to tie into bundles before it shatters in handling, and the bundles stored open to air until well dried. Then it can be gathered into bundles as large as your hand can hold, tied with cotton string. I like to use four colors of string to honor the Grandmothers and Grandfathers of the Four Directions—red for East (dawn), yellow for south, black for the west (twilight), and white for north (snow). Make a loop in the string or strings to tie the end with the thickest stems and spiral the longer strings around the bundle to the opposite end and back to tie to the strings around the base. Be sure to allow the bundles to dry in the open for a few more days in a dry location to avoid mold.

A natural container is needed to hold the sage while it burns or smolders. I like a medium-size clamshell to honor the animal people, or an Earthenware pot or a hollowed rock which would honor the rocks and waters. You will need a way to fan the embers to keep them burning or smoldering. In some traditions, it is considered disrespectful to blow upon the smudge with one's breath. You can use your hand to sweep air to the embers, but a feather, feather fan, or wing are much more effective. To start or relight smudge you may also need matches or a lighter.

You can use this ceremony to cleanse people, places, and things. Smudging brings awareness of the sacred and should be performed with sensitivity and respect. As you add each pinch of the smudge mixture to the shell or pot, offer thanks to the Grandmothers and Grandfathers of the Four Directions—the order of honoring might differ from nation to nation. Some start with the east because that is sunrise (until the pole reversal, that is), Mother Earth, up to honor Father Sky, to your heart, over your head, over each shoulder, and over your heart. With the help of another, the bottoms of your feet, up and down each leg, and across your back. Pass through the smoke whatever ceremonial instrument is to be used: drums, beaters, pipe, your hands, or a dreamcatcher.

When the ceremony is complete, the ashes should be totally buried (avoid using more than you need) or otherwise respectfully returned to Mother Earth, never dumped into garbage or trash. The purpose of the Medicine Path is to always walk in beauty, in balance between ego and heart, honoring the Great Mystery within you and All That Is, and respecting All Beings in the Web of Life.

Although you might prefer to pray from your own heart, here is a sample prayer:

Grandmothers and Grandfathers of the East, each day you bring new light so that we may grow in knowledge and wisdom. We have been waiting for the time when your light would shine in the hearts of all people, that they would remember the Original Instructions that were written in our hearts since the beginning of all things.

Grandmothers and Grandfathers of the South, your warm winds have sent us your love and abundance from Mother Earth. We have always known that as we follow the Original Instructions, we will walk in balance and harmony and all our needs will be met. The power and wisdom of this path is not easily understood when we teach our mind inside boundaries and the heart is closed to sissagwad, the soft wind of spirit. Open the heart of those who follow the way of the mind.

Grandmothers and Grandfathers of the West, in the darkness of night you have sent us dreams to see deep inside our hearts, to learn how to walk the path of spirit. We see the beauty that hides behind each moment and discover the Great Mystery that is in us and all things. Help the people of the mind see the power of their dreams so that they can remember the Original instructions.

Grandmothers and Grandfathers of the North, you have brought us the cold winds and snows each year to cleanse our Mother Earth. Now the cleansing of the mind has begun. The energies of the stars have shifted into a new focus to end domination and hierarchy. No longer is it possible to live by the mind alone unless it is guided by the heart. Blow the fresh, clean wind of spirit to sweep away the belief systems that limit our brothers and sisters who are trapped in the way of the mind.

Kee-shay Giidgii Manidou, you have sent visions and dreams to help us remember Who We Are. We have not forgotten the Original Instructions. The stories have now been rediscovered and returned to the people. You have shown that the path of reconciliation and peace is through the heart. Send the light of inspiration to the Ogichidaag' who will show others a new way of being.

Gee-mama-nama-kee, you are our Mother, our Source of Life. You have provided us our food, our water, air, shelter and so many beautiful beings who are our Brothers and Sisters. We know we are connected to you and all other beings in the Web of Life. Many are those who do not see this connection. They see with only their eyes and their mind. With a narrow focus they see parts of things instead of the energy of love and wholeness. They have forgotten the Original Instructions. As their Mother you have been patient with them. Extend that patience a little longer so the Ogichi-daag' can show them a new way.

Great Mystery, we feel your presence in us and in all things. You are the spiral energy of love that connects all, is all. You are the Circle of Life, the circle way, the Original Instructions. When we are living in our heart, we can soar with the White Eagle to see beyond horizons of heart and mind.

In smudge offerings to the Four Directions, we are centering and bringing our being into balance and creating a circle that separates the sacred from the profane—a ritual that sets the trance state apart from the ordinary waking consciousness, making a space that can be entered and exited, structuring a sacred energy pattern that will contain, focus, and amplify the ritual whether it is journeying, drumming, or praying.

The spirals danced and swirled.
"Oh, how I love the fragrance of sage," sang a Grandmother as she spun around a cloud.
"It's good to know that those experiencing body remember those of us who did that before," smiled a Grandfather. "But then, I vaguely remember how frustrating it was to tie my shoes."
"And it's such a joy to help them learn," winked a Grandmother, "and help them make the connections they planned to complete their journeys."
"Especially when they recognize connections that are their own plans for their space and time experience," chortled the Dreamkeeper. "That seems to surprise them every time!"
"So strange that many remember nothing, and some remember just enough to be surprised," sang a laughing Grandmother.
The Spirals whirled and chanted.

Shamanic Drumming

The drum used in some ceremonies of the Ojibwe, especially the men in a Midewiwin sweat lodge, is the water drum, made from a log of basswood about 16 inches long and about 10 inches wide that has been hollowed by slowly burning, charring, and scraping. A thin wooden disk is fitted into the lower end, a small hole bored part way up one side and plugged. The head of the drum is a heavy, tanned deer hide at least 18 inches in diameter.

A few inches of water are poured in when the drum is to be used, the hide is wet, wrung out, laid over the open top and stretched by a hoop made from a willow sapling, wound with a cloth or hide pressed down to tighten the deer hide head. When not in use, the water can be removed by unplugging the hole in the side. If the head becomes too dry, it can be moistened by splashing remaining water inside or by sprinkling a handful of water over the top. If too damp, the drum can be exposed to the sun until it tightens. The water in the drum makes a low sound that can be heard 10 miles away. Special drumming sticks are usually carved to represent the loon, and some have a curved end with a cushion of deer hide to give a softer sound."[CC96]

You can become your own teacher, priest, prophet and healer, bringing ultimate power over your own life and to help others do the same. A shaman enters an altered state of consciousness by meditation, T'ai Chi, dancing, or drumming to make journeys into alternate realities, seeking the knowledge and power that resides in those worlds. These methods and the awareness that follows have withstood the tests of time, varying little from one culture to another. An entire life path develops in which everything is based on relationships in which all life forms are integrated and interdependent. The shaman is aware of these interrelationships and serves as an intermediary on behalf of his own community. The shaman seeks harmony and balance with the natural world and his drum serves as an instrument of attunement.

I recommend a 16 inch diameter shaman drum close to 2 inches deep so you can reach the backside with the forefinger or thumb to add a variety of extra sounds you can create. I like deer hide for the drumhead and birch or cedar for the frame. My drum also has a stone in the handgrip to represent the rocks and waters in the Four Orders of Being, along with hide representing the Animals, the wood frame representing the plants, and me representing the humans. These are the Four Orders of Being in the Web of Life, each interwoven with the others, interconnected in the One. To represent the underworld and sky world, the drumhead can be painted in halves, one half representing the sky world and the opposite half, the under world. Mine represents the Great Mystery.

The shamanic drum opens greater opportunities to experience the mysterious world of the shaman. It requires no faith. In fact shamanism, like Gnosticism, is more about Knowing than believing. As I mentioned before, shaman is a word from the Northern Asia Manchu-Tungus word šaman, meaning 'one who knows', whereas 'Gnosis' derives from the Greek meaning 'to know through experience'. The drum will awaken the shaman that is in you. The drum rhythm connects the shaman to the rhythms of the universe. Rhythm is the universal language, the heartbeat of the universe, promoting individual and planetary resonance.

If you have a drum, and it has not been opened by a shaman, and you can't locate a shaman near you, you can smudge yourself and then smudge your drum and drumstick. Then gently beat on it and say this prayer, in English:

> I seek the drum,
> Upon my drum bestow the mystery,
> (And to All that is.)
> Thanks, Great Spirit,
> It is so.

or in Anishaabemowin, the language of the Anishinabeg (Ojibway):

> M'day-wewe-wigun, nindo-wiyauh
> N'miday wewe-wigun,
> man-i-tou-wiyaunwi-wih
> (toward Ishpeming—heaven)
> M'gwech Giidji manidou.
> Kiki-nowautchi-beegaudae.

You can and should create your own prayers and songs by listening to your own heart. You do not need to learn Ojibwe, or any other Native American language to sing or pray. Most important is to be authentically YOU, not authentically Ojibwe or Indian.

I was fortunate to have been invited to a conference where an Ojibway shaman had been invited. During a break, I gave him a pouch of tobacco and asked him if he would open my drum. He agreed, and opened my drum in the traditional ceremony. I might not be so fortunate again, but I recognized the difficulty of finding another shaman so far from the Reservations in Minnesota and time is of the essence. We must quickly learn and practice what is needed, and I might have to do it myself.

If your drum has been opened you now must learn to listen to the sissagwad, the soft wind of spirit that whispers in your heart. Your heart is a powerful source of wisdom that is often bullied by an egoic mind. In a later chapter there are meditations and heart-oriented ceremonies that will help you balance or improve the contribution that your heart can make to your shamanic life. Listen to the sissagwad in your heart. You don't need to get locked into any rigid ritual. That's a head thing, an ego-mind thing. Please don't misunderstand—the mind is good, but the tendency in our common culture is that the ego-mind is too often allowed to rule over the heart, losing a valuable function of the heart. The heart is much more than a mere pump. We are beginning to understand what indigenous people have known for a very long time, how the heart may be where the soul speaks. Learning to contrast the distinct codes of heart and mind, we may be able to recognize more easily which of our cultural artifacts are serving the objectives of the more selfish brain and which promote the more altruistic agenda of the heart.[HC26]

Ground yourself by sitting with a straight spine, head held high, still your mind, and breathe deeply. Feel the Earth energy meet the cosmic energy flowing down into the top of your head to meet at your heart. Energy cardiology and cardio-energetics provide a starting point for scientists who meet with healers, kahuna, shamans, and all those who seek to be re-enchanted by the energy of their heart and lessons of their cellular memories.[HC 61] Heart, step up to center stage and take a bow.

When you are grounded, you form a sense of intent from your heart that is specific, enlightening, healing, and guiding, all flowing from the Great Mystery. Start the drumming in high tones by pressing your thumb up against the back of the drumhead. Allow the drum to guide you in tempo and overtones. When you have received the gifts from the Great Mystery, give thanks by drumming in the high tones. If you journey, you might be able to enter the quantum world beyond time and space that has been so wondrously described by those who have had near-death experiences.

Listening to the soft wind of spirit in your heart is an awesome source of wisdom beyond anything of which the brain is capable. One of the ceremonial uses of the shamanic drum is healing. The first time I used the drum in healing I heard the sissagwad whisper to me to hold the drum over each chakra and beat softly. It worked!

The next time I was asked to do healing, I did some energy work on chakras by a gentle massage to break up blockages as I had been instructed to do by listening to my heart. Then I noticed my drum nearby and realized I was being instructed to use it… but not by beating it. I was instructed by the sissagwad to caress the drum to make the sound of the wind whipping up a storm. Then I used my fingernails scraping across the drum to make the sound of thunder. Drawing my fingers across the drum with more pressure to imitate lightning, I let the thunder and lightning disappear into the distance. With more wind and lingering thunder and lightning came the rain with the tapping of fingers making the sound of a multitude of raindrops striking the ground. More wind, more rain, a bit more distant thunder and lightning, the rainstorm diminished to silence with a gentle wind… the hurts and pains had been washed away and all was fresh and healed.

Another time, a friend in Denver asked me to help with one of her horses that had a wound that would not heal. I thought, *OK, some sage ceremony, some drumming.*

I heard the sissagwad, "Not drumming. Use the rattle."

"What?" I questioned.

The sissagwad repeated, "Not drumming. Use the rattle."

"Impossible!" I thought. I remembered the cowboy movies I saw as a boy. The horse hears the snake rattling and panics, rearing high in the air, and I'm going to be right there under the flailing hooves!

"How about drumming instead," I begged.

"Not drumming. Use the rattle."

I did the sage ceremony, smudging the entire paddock and the horse. The horse stood perfectly still as I began to shake the rattle by each leg, tentatively, watchful of any hint of a dangerous response. None. It worked! Then the horse 'whispered' to me that 'it had tickled.'

"What?" I asked.

"It tickled," the horse repeated. "When she took the bandage off too soon, it still tickled, so I scratched it."

I told Diana to keep the wrap on a little longer and the problem was solved.

A few months later my friends in Fargo surprised me when they took me see a new movie just out, *The Horse Whisperer,* but I knew that it worked both ways—the horse can whisper to the human, too.

People are drawn to drums for varied reasons, almost always the work of some deeper wisdom or Mystery. Group drumming has been shown by a team of MDs led by Barry Bittman, M.D., to increases cancer-killing cells, which help the body combat not only cancer, but other viruses, including AIDS. "Group drumming tunes our biology, orchestrates our immunity, and enables healing to begin… When our hands connect to a drum that unites with our energy, vitality… and unity, we become whole again."

This new medical research follows recent biofeedback research showing that even brief heartbeat-mimicking drumming can double alpha waves, a light meditative brain wave and reduce stress. We know that stress depresses the immune system and has been linked to nearly all diseases. Drumming has also been used successfully with Alzheimer's patients to focus attention, with war veterans to end PTSD, with addicts in recovery from drug and alcohol abuse, and with prison and homeless populations to enhance self-esteem. Even corporations such as Motorola, AT&T, and Levi-Strauss have used drumming to promote team spirit-building. Widely published research also indicates that playing musical instruments increases kid's learning abilities. This appears especially true of those instruments that can be played intuitively, like drums.

Qualitative studies have shown that drumming enhances right-brain functions of intuition and creativity. The drum's pulse synchronizes the left and right hemispheres of the brain. When these hemispheres begin to pulsate in harmony, there is a change in the physiology of the brainwaves that produces a heightened awareness, expanded into the ecstatic state, the divine octave of resonance called the Rainbow Bridge by the Cherokee. This happens when left and right brains are in resonance, renewing the flow of the intuitive mind.[TSD 22]

The brain's fundamental need for rhythm has long been known in the field of musical therapy. Clinical studies demonstrate the stress produced when the brain is deprived of this basic need. The effect of stress upon the human system has now been incontrovertibly established: stress contributes to all disease and is a primary cause of a myriad life-threatening illnesses, such as heart attacks, strokes, and immune system breakdowns. Many healers believe that stress is a result of psychic fragmentation, of being disconnected from our deeper selves.

A study by Barry Quinn, PhD, a clinical psychologist specializing in neuro-biofeedback for stress management, indicates that drumming for brief periods can change brainwave patterns, dramatically reducing stress. 30-40 minutes of drumming has been shown to double the Alpha brainwaves, which promote mental relaxation. Music therapist Barry Bernstein, whose use of the drum with Alzheimer's patients as well as in corporate settings, believes strongly that drumming "is the healthiest, most accessible and fastest way to reconnect with ourselves."

Care Of The Drum

Storage—Let your drum live where you live. Storing it wrapped up or enclosed for extended periods of time will relax the hide.

Extreme Temperatures—When traveling, protect your drum by wrapping it in a blanket or putting it in its drum bag to insulate the drum from wide fluctuations in temperature and humidity. Never leave your drum in a closed automobile in the sun, near a fire or heating vent or any heat source. Doing so may cause the hide to crack!

High Humidity—If the hide on your drum relaxes due to high humidity, it will return to its original tension if it has not been over-heated. A hide drumhead will change its sound as the weather changes. This can be quite natural. The more you rub, handle, and play your drum the more your natural oils penetrate the hide, thus lengthening its life and enriching it. For this reason, it is traditionally not shared with others and not ace meets the wood.

You should also oil your drum with Neatsfoot Oil every few months applied to the back of the hide and around the holes where the lace meets the wood.

While you drum, you can chant or sing a prayer that is carried to the spirit world on the echo of the drum. Don't worry about the language, they have plenty of interpreters at hand, so to speak. Besides, the language of the heart is universal—infinite and eternal.

Listen to the sissagwad in your heart. Do not get yourself locked into rigid rituals. That's a head thing, a mind thing. Another way to use the drum is to create a buzzing sound by touching the back side of the drumhead with tip of a fingernail or fingertip for a softer sound. Medicine men will often place inside the drum a stick with several smaller sticks pressing lightly against the back of the drumhead. The multiple tones and harmonics can elicit healing. Unlike the medicine drum, you can withdraw your fingernail from the backside of the drumhead to create a normal beat. With a little practice you might be able to get the drum to emit a high frequency harmonic that sings and reaches deeply into the heart. You can also use the tip of your finger to create a stop to a beat and therefore create many new rhythm possibilities. You can use the fingernail of your forefinger to scratch on the backside of the drumhead in counter rhythm to the drumbeat, or you can press against the backside of the drumhead to change the tone of the drum, giving it another voice.

Using and combining these drumming techniques, you have a diverse vocabulary of sounds that you can use as needed. If your fingers are long enough you might even be able to use both thumb and forefinger, giving you two variations on the backside of the drumhead. Your virtuosity is not limited to a change of volume and rhythms. You will also find it very dramatic and powerful to strike the drumhead hard with the beater and then hold the beater firmly against the drumhead. It is almost like an explosion and reverberates with a rising, ringing tone. Used with a crescendo of volume and rhythm, you can punctuate the finale of a sequence or, followed with a softer drumming and nuanced rhythms, you can create a symphony in percussion. The thin design of the shamanic drum makes this virtuosity possible.

There are many ways to use the drum for sending prayers, for connecting to the Star Web. It also allows you to receive power, wisdom, and healing energy. As you discover your natural heritage of power and wisdom, the drum can be used to remove blockages of energy flow, wash away residues of hurt and pain, and lift you into other worlds. Learn the power of deep passion, the carrier wave of love and healing.

Your drum can teach you to listen to the whisper of the spirit wind in your heart. Some people call this meditation, but it is simply connecting with Mother Earth and Father Sky, the Starweb, the Grandmothers and Grandfathers who are the Spiritkeepers of the Four Directions, and most importantly, with the Great Mystery that abides within you. These are the Seven Directions. The shamanic journey takes people to an experience of consciousness where they can use energies around them to heal themselves, the sun, and the Milky Way Galaxy. The shamanic journey can help bring the 'whole cosmos' back into balance. This includes physical health and emotional well-being, giving people the strength to make meaningful changes while feeling in resonance through their connection with the energies around them.

Drumming for healing of our Sun as it approaches micronova might avoid some of the worst effects and lead to more people surviving so we can continue the wisdom of the heart as expressed by shamanic and Gnostic people.

Make smudge offerings and pray for harmony and balanced energy. Begin drumming near the high pitch part of the drumhead, near the edge or press upward with a finger or thumb from under the drumhead to create a higher pitch. Use a rapid, eagle heartbeat (180-200 beats/minute) and singing into the drum to ask eagle to carry any dark energy you find or feel, far away into the stars to be dropped into a hot star where it can be transformed or transmuted.

When you feel this has been done then switch the drumbeat to a lower pitch drumbeat nearer the center of the drum. This will bring that transformed energy back to you and you ground it through your root chakra at the end of your spine. Switch to a high pitch drumbeat as before. Thank the eagle, all your relations, the animal world, plant world, and the rocks and waters.

In a drumming circle, 10 people of like mind have the power of 100 individuals, so even a small group of one-mind-one-heart can transform the world and manifest a healing of the Earth-Sun system to bring about change in what is coming and in each of you.

It is OK to pray for healing Mother Earth and Father Sun. They are alerting us to the cleansing and purification they need. The Sun is no longer yellow—it's almost white. The magnetic poles are rapidly moving. The magnetic north had been moving about 5 miles a year and now is moving more than 5 miles a month. It had been in northern Canada for a long time, then suddenly headed for the North Geographic Pole and crossed the Arctic Ocean to northern Siberia. The South Magnetic Pole has left Antarctica and is headed north. Healing the Earth-Sun must begin with our own cleansing and purification.

We receive life-force energy from Father Sun and Mother Earth. They both meet in the heart. The drum attunes us and our world. Mother Earth turns because of that energy flow from Father Sun. When the North and

South poles flip, our magnetic shield that protects us from high energies like cosmic rays and gamma rays, suddenly disappears for a while. With the rotation of the planet, water from oceans, seas, and lakes slops over the shores and tsunamis race across the continents. Once upon a time, native people knew it was their responsibility to maintain a balance of Earth energies, but when they were removed from their lands, the people who had organized their removal knew nothing of the essential ceremonies and rituals that kept the land balanced.

Drumming in the star world high pitch edge of the drum at the eagle-heartbeat rate (180-200 beats/minute) and singing into the drum to ask eagle to change and balance negative thoughts and energies, then focus balanced and transmuted energy to heal Mother Earth and Father Sky by drumming a prayer of healing, singing into an eagle-heartbeat in the high pitch zone of the drumhead at the edge, or where you raise a thumb or finger on the underside of the drum. Then switch the drumming to the lower pitch spot and focus your attention to your lower spine to deliver energy to Mother Earth and Father Sun. Switch to a high pitch drumbeat as before. Thank the eagle and all your relations, the animal world, plant world, and the rocks and waters.

The time of Cleansing will come soon. The Earth and Sun have done this cataclysmic dance many times before. How destructive the cleansing will depend upon how many humans change their attitudes toward Mother Earth and Father Sky, and live in harmony and balance, and ask for wisdom that you might live."[SD 70]

Listening To Whispers In The Heart

I didn't go looking for it.
It found me
in the busyness of the day.

I was quiet.
I've learned to be quiet,
at peace in the most chaotic places.

Just doing what I do—I listen
to the whispers in the heart,
wisps of thought in the mind,
the spirit wind that whispers in the heart.

It's hard to explain.
I don't know if it can be explained,
but it's there. It happens.
I just listen.

aaheart+++

The Now Moment

A clear glass marble demonstrates a reality of life on Earth. It was for such an experience you chose to come here to this realm of time and space. Each of your experiences in this finite world of time and space is a precious gift, a treasure of great value. This is especially true of your problems… and even your tragedies. Inside the mysteries of each moment is a new way to learn and grow. Each of these glass marbles is an experience of the Now Moment.

- The past is always clouded by opinion and judgements.
- The future is hidden in the mist of free choice and fantasy.
- The Now Moment is perfectly clear.
- The past is dead.
- The future is not yet born.
- Only in the Now Moment do you truly experience LIFE!
- You cannot dance in what was.
- You cannot sing in what will be.

- Only in the Now Moment can you taste the beauty of All That Is.
- The past is always ending.
- The future is always beginning.
- Each Now Moment simply IS.
- Only in the Now Moment can you know the Great Mystery within.
- Only in the Now Moment can you remember your Original Instructions.
- Place your Now Moment in the light and look into the windows of your heart.
- There you will find power and wisdom, strength and gentleness, peace and vision.

Carry a Now Moment in your pocket, in your purse or bag. Put it on a vacant part of your desk where you can notice it often during the day.

All day long you can touch it and remember that only the Now Moment is REAL. This is central to what is to follow in the rest of this book.

Place a bowl of Now Moments on your table or desk. If someone asks, tell them the story of the Now Moment.

- Give a Now Moment to a friend who is stuck in the past or the future.
- Or, to a stranger who needs a vision of hope, a possibility of peace.
- Tell them what you've learned about the Now Moment.
- Give them a Now Moment to help them remember.
- Gnosticism is rooted firmly in the Now Moment.[LJ 130]

* * *

Gnosticism is an investigation of the Now Moment. Gnosis is a state of awakening that arises when you examine a Now Moment and become conscious of what you are actually knowing right now. It's not about believing —it's about KNOWING! What IS this NOW Moment? What does it feel like to be alive? Can you feel a rush of excitement as you become conscious of the awesome mystery of existence? The stories we tell about life. A NOW Moment is a precious gift. Love the fact that you EXIST at this Now Moment. What a miracle Life IS! LIFE is a breath-taking mystery and it is magical.

> If your mind is your master,
> you are in forever bondage
> to an abusive past
> you think you remember.
> Or in fear of an unhappy future
> that doesn't exist.
> The Now Moment merely IS—infinite possibility.
> Live Here Now!
>
> aaheart+++

You exist! Focus on this miracle! Focus your attention on the Mystery of THIS moment, and you could feel profoundly ALIVE! Sometimes we tend to take this experience of existence for granted. You exist RIGHT NOW! Each sight, each sound is unique and unbelievably stunning! And you are HERE to see it, you are here to hear it! All you need is to be AWARE of it! CONSCIOUS of it! Savor it. There's one thing that's always NOW! You are always!

* * *

I AM the melody of a song
that sings of truth and love
you are the staff and note and key,
the beat and rhythm from above.

This song is yours to sing along.
the music is yours to Be.
a gift from Mother/Father spirits
to know eternity.

Your path and mine
will share this song
however long this mile,
and when we've found a silence deep
we'll dance the stars a while
and waft the Fragrance of truth and Love
to those whose spirits sleep.

Awake, arise!
their day begun,
to the truth of WHO they are,
to be and know that they are one,
Sons and Daughters of a star.

aaheart+++

The Grandmothers and Grandfathers danced the Spirals a while. "We spiral around. We spiral around, as Spirits of the Earth."

Shamanic/Gnostic Poetry

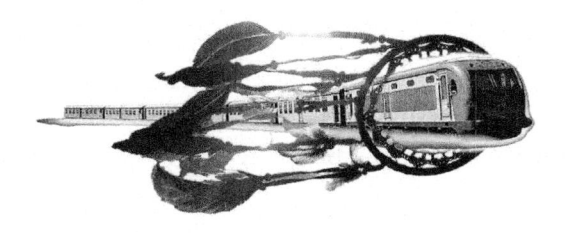

Wake up, wake up
you sleepy head!

Rouse yourself from the collective coma you mistake for life.¹¹³ See through the illusion of separateness. Recognize we are all one. There is ONE awareness dreaming itself to be everyone and everything. The simple secret to enjoying this dream we call life is to wake up to oneness. When we are very focused in the life-dream you seem to be a person within the world, but when you become conscious of your true nature as awareness, you start to live lucidly so you recognize the world exists within you. The thoughts you are thinking at this very moment have their existence within YOU. This book you are holding exists because of your awareness. As a body you are an object that exists in the world, but as awareness you are an infinite emptiness which can and does, contain the world.

Get up, get up,
get out of bed!

***

Knowing you are one with all, you will find yourself in love with all… and fall in love with being. This was the message of the original Christians. They symbolized this awakened state with the enigmatic 'laughing Jesus.' The Original Christians were inspired men and women who saw how beautiful life could be if we would wake up and live in love. WHO you truly are "is not at all in time or place, but is purely and simply in eternity" as Meister Eckhart phrases it. As awareness you don't exist in time, time exists in you. You are awareness witnessing the flow of appearances we call 'time'.

Live, love, laugh, and be happy!

Those who have cast ignorance aside, as if awakening from sleep, no longer see the world as real. Gnosis, valued as though it were the dawn of a new awareness, no longer portrays the world as real, but like a dream at night. Gnosis is like waking up. Gnostics are those awakened to the reality of oneness.—Gospel of Truth, Nag Hamadi Codex.

In the Gospel of Thomas, Jesus proclaims that if you understand the teachings of awakening you will "not taste death." Does that mean that gnosis makes you immortal? No. Gnosis is becoming conscious that you are already immortal and always have been. It's your nature. Who you are was never born. What you are was born and will die, but who you are and always have been, was never born. You are the awareness which watched birth, and which one day will witness its death. But awareness does not age or die. It is a permanent presence within which the life dream is arising.

The body exists in time and space and has a use by date, so the body has a limited shelf-life. Who you are is eternal and infinite, beyond time and space.

***

First sung by Al Jolson in 1949, written by Harry Woods in 1926. Fundamentals of Gnosticism in a happy popular tune.

> Dreamkeeper,
> my eyes wish to see
> behind the face of me.
>
> My ears wish to hear
> the song of my beginning.
>
> Show me the hidden worlds
> behind, beyond, within.
>
> I Am More than I seem—
> I Am the Dreamer of Dreams.
>
> aaheart+++

Dreamkeepers, dreams, hidden worlds are shamanic and Gnostic because they seek to unveil mystery and illusion. Acknowledging **I AM more than I seem** is an end result of the seeking, inquiring mind of the Gnostic. Gnostics interpret their teachings as signposts pointing to the experience of awakening. We bring the ancient Gnostic teachings to life using modern language and vernacular, fresh without unfamiliar religious mumbo-jumbo. We want you to get the cosmic joke and laugh with us, understanding why the Gnostic Jesus laughs with us.[LJ 9] There is only the life-dreamer dreaming the life-dream.[LJ 173]

Warrior Of The Light—Gnosis

WHO you Are is a Warrior of the Light,
a co-creator whose wisdom and power
is One with the Creator.

This is your natural state of being,
what you are is a human being
that has forgotten WHO he is
and is searching for his true identity.

Beliefs urge you to do this or that.
You focus on doing
and you accumulate deeds,
accomplishments, things,
control over others,
more and more WHAT
that hides WHO
under a mountain of doing.

To find your natural freedom
you will have to let go of constant doing
and your belief in doing.

WHO you are does not depend upon
what you have and what you do.
Then you will find the natural beauty
of WHO you Are.

Therefore, you can say of yourself—
I AM OGICHIDAG'.
(a spirit leader of the People)

* * *

Even a tree has a subtle sense of awareness,
a Self-awareness.
Imagine the courage it would take
to live an entire life on the rim of a gorge,
each year your roots would reach even deeper
into the crack in the rock searching
for more nutrients and water
and each year your roots widen the crack in the rock
until one day your grip on life would be loosened
and you plunge into the abyss.

Is this a tragedy?

Consider WHO you Are—
The WHAT of you would become food
for the beetles, worms, and fungi.
The WHAT of you would recombine with All That IS.

Does the WHAT of you disappear?
Or does it simply take a new form?
Does the WHO of you disappear
upon the death of the WHAT? WHO IS.

WHAT only appears to be.
Without WHAT, WHO IS.

WHAT has a beginning, so WHAT ends.
WHO is beginningless,
so, WHO never ends.

* * *

Knowing this you can live in freedom and joy.
It takes courage to let go of the WHAT
to live as though your WHAT
is simply an expression of WHO you Are.

Live joyfully here and now knowing
that 'WHAT' is WHO'S field of play.

Although WHAT you are is
birth and death without end,
WHO you Are is beyond all limitation—
Infinite and eternal,
Beyond space and time.

aaheart+++

Beyond space and time is eternity and infinity, worlds not readily apparent to the uninitiated. We aren't characters in this soap opera, we're safely watching the show from the cheap seats in the balcony, or up close and personal, however we choose to play it. The irony is that the more we identify with our apparent nature as a person (WHAT) the more scared of life we become, but the more we know we are really not that person in the soap opera, the more we can play a part in the life process, confident that no matter how daunting, we are secure and safe to surf the adventure of life as the indomitable WHO.[LJ 167] You have a dual nature. You appear to be a person (WHAT), but essentially, you are awareness, consciousness, itself (WHO).

Love is the answer and you know that for sure.
Love is a flower. You got to let it, you gotta let it grow.
~John Lennon—Lyrics © Downtown Music Publishing

Gnostic poets know that Love is the answer, the goal and result of Gnosis. The purpose of life is to love being in this moment. Driven by other desires, you miss the point and identify with the life dream, lost in the experience instead of being the experiencer. Somewhere deep in all of us, we DO know that through our consciousness we are all connected—connected, for sure. We might be energetically connected through our heart energy that keeps us in hidden communication. Carl Jung calls it, the Collective Unconscious. On some subtle level, all information gathered by those who have gone before, may still be non-locally represented in the memory system of every cell of our own body. Being less brain-infatuated and more alert to subtle info-energy being resonated with every beat of the heart may be like tuning a radio to the station that contains our collective cellular memory program." [THC 153]

So, when I have need of knowing,
I tweak my radio dial,
tune in the needed broadcast
and wear my knowing smile.

Red, this living morning light,
hours after dawn.
Our Sun has crossed the magic line
that gathers close the night,
to meet the Moon and share the sky,
merging into one.

The dimming of the day affords
the brilliant flash of starry sport
as all around me flames cavort

and dance the rhythms of the stars.

My soul and body tuned
with a dark and blazing Moon,
I AM One in the loving Cosmic Heart.

MY dreams awake,
the Breath of Sleep,
to stir my Being as I make
my pilgrimage
through sunlit deep,
until I find my home aright
in starbright heavens
of the night.

aaheart+++

Awakening to oneness is the experience of big love. Knowing you are one with all, you find yourself in love with all. As awareness you are spacious emptiness which contains the world and the universe. You are a timeless presence which witnesses the flow of experiences we call time.[IJ 226] We are really 'stardust.' We've arisen from before the cosmos so we could truly consider ourselves to be 'cosmopolitan.' We are one human family, and the universe is our Mother.[IJ 208]

We are the WHO of consciousness that is aware that WHAT 'matters.'

The Unbroken Circle

The circle represents the unbroken wholeness
from which we draw our power and strength.
It is our Source of being.

Everything is in the circle.
Within the circle, traditional people
follow their ancient ways of connection
to each other and to Mother Earth.

At the center of All That Is
the Creator weaves the Web of Life,
spiraling from the known to the unknown.
Our life travels a spiral path
of co-creativity and co-creation, with the Creator.
Four orders of being—rocks, water and air;
trees, grasses, and flowers;
four-legged, winged, swimmers, and crawlers;
and the two-legged, the human—
We all depend on each other.

aaheart+++

Gnostics have been proposing this BIG idea for millennia. All is One. Life is one awareness becoming conscious of itself in infinitely various forms, and to embrace this is an experience of all-embracing love.[IJ 213-214] Life is a just a dream, sweetheart. Hello, hello again. Here's hoping that we'll meet again. Sh-Boom! Sh-Boom! Life is a dream we are co-creating as we become more conscious. Gnostics keep alive the dream of Heaven on Earth.[IJ 210]

Dream After A Dream

One dream after another,
the Dreamkeeper fills your sleep
with dreams
to show your connection
to all that is.

If you listen with your heart
instead of your mind,
what sounds true
is simply a reminder
of what you already know.

Sift the wheat from the chaff
on the wind of your soul.
Walk your own path
in truth and beauty
following your dreams,
one dream after another.

           aaheart+++

The foibles which keep you unconscious in the life-dream are your qualities which have become distorted because you presume yourself to be an isolated individual WHAT.[LJ 227] Science is the study of the life-dream. Gnosticism is the art of waking up to WHO you really are.[LJ 129] Recognize You are the spacious emptiness of awareness within which the life-dream is arising.[LJ 172] Gnosticism is Knowing that life is good, and death is safe.[LJ 164]

The good news is there is a natural state of happiness which is our birthright.[JLG 3]

Gnosis is not an intellectual theory. Gnosis is a state of being, inner knowledge. Quantum Knowing, gnosis, is a realization, here and now, of our true identity, WHO was never born and so can never die.[JLG 5]

Much that is written in Pagan books is found also in the books of God's Church. That which they share in common are the words that spring from the heart, the law that is inscribed on the heart—Valentinus, Gnostic poet, 100-180 CE, author of the Gospel of Truth found buried in a vase in the desert at Nag Hamadi.

We are not a physical body that is sometimes conscious. We are Consciousness (WHO) that is sometimes conscious of a body (WHAT). In the dream-state, we abandon the body (WHAT) and retreat into the psyche or soul. In the deep sleep state we withdraw completely into our essence as nous/pneuma, spirit of Consciousness (WHO), conscious of nothing.[JLG 61]

Twin Towers Of Tragedy

When she fell
she could not know
the Mystery she held,
that from the Littlest Acorn
a mighty oak would grow,
that what she thought was tragedy
had only set her free
to be the Forest's gift of love,
the powerful Woman tree.

Inside the chrysalis
He could not know
The mystery he held,
that from a homely caterpillar
a butterfly would grow,
that what he thought was tragedy
had only set him free
to be the Meadow's gift of love,
the wings of liberty.

aaheart+++

The unfolding of the acorn to realize the hidden reality of the majestic giant of the forest, the powerful woman tree, and the unveiling of the meadow's gift of love, the wings of liberty, both represent the unveiling of Consciousness as WHO we truly are, Creation's gift of love, our immortality. The great revelation of Gnosticism is that our essential identity is Consciousness.[JLG 61] Both the Littlest Acorn and the caterpillar underwent a transformation toward transcendental Being, WHO.

***

Angels Of The Light

There was only light
and radiant waves of love
We were the light, we were Love,
and we were One.

We were a magnificent,
glowing, loving Sun
sending forth Our Light to All
so the Universe would know
eternal Truth
held by the Wisdom of Love,
the Love that I AM,
the Love that We Are,
light from a glowing, loving Star.

The Power of our Love
blazed intense and bright.
Our Star could no longer contain
the Love and Light
and We became many.

We were magnificent, glowing,
loving Angels
carrying forth to All, Our Star
so the universe would know
eternal Wisdom,
embraced by the Truth of Love—

the Love that I AM,
the Love that We Are.
Light from a glowing, loving Star.

In the depth of Love, we came
to save this world from inner Death,
to transmute matter into Light,
to lift its low vibration
beyond the dark of Night
and spare this icy, denser realm,
its plunging, hopeless flight.

In giving so much Light and Love
we've nearly all forgot
our magnificent, glowing, starry past
believing what we're not.

And now we must remember
the Truth of WHO WE ARE,
Angel Beings co-creating,
Sons and Daughters of a Star.

We are magnificent,
glowing, loving Children
of a nearly forgotten Sun
Whose Light goes forth to brighten All
so the world would know it's One,
enfolded by the power of Love,
the Love that I AM,
the Love that We Are,
light from a glowing, loving Star.

aaheart+++

* * *

Gnosis is the knowledge that all is One.[JLG 73] As the dazzling darkness—the center in itself—we are the universal Beings the Gnostics call God.[JLG 61] The Consciousness of God is the dazzling darkness.[JLG 65] The magical quality that we associate with dreams starts to breakout in our everyday experience. Mundane reality (WHAT) becomes strangely mythic and meaningfully WHO.[JLG 74] The Father is the Great Mystery—the dazzling darkness of unconscious Consciousness.[JLG 75] In the Gospel of Matthew 5:14 Jesus teaches his disciples: "You are the lights of the cosmos."

> Stars a-borning
> we take flight
> to find the morning
> of our night,
> to ride the lifestream
> of our day,
> and dance a new dream
> on our way
> to journey far beyond what seems,
> beyond the worlds of our dreams.
>
> aaheart+++

All stars shine because of one light. All individual consciousnesses are the flaring forth of the dazzling darkness.[JLG 127] Consciousness (WHO) dreams the dream of the cosmos and identifies with all the different characters within the dream.[JLG 135]

"Time is the evolving cosmos, which is ever laboring to bring the ideal, planning to lead all to an unending state of excellence."—Plotinus[JLG 137]

***

Consciousness (WHO) is the fundamental concept at the heart of Gnostic metaphysics because it is the prerequisite for existence.[JLG 131] Consciousness dreams the dream of the cosmos and identifies with all of the different characters within the dream (WHAT).[JLG 139] We are part of the evolving cosmos.[JLG 141] Without our awareness, the cosmos would not exist.

> I Am a Child of God's Universe,
> Through my eyes the Stars can see.
> The brightness of a billion suns
> the Cosmos knows through me.
> I am the Light of Peace

You are not a separate individual with free will, because everything is happening as an integral part of the ever-changing life-dream, including 'your' thoughts and actions… sight is God seeing through your eyes.'[JLG 173]

Body-Mind-Spirit

If we see ourselves as body,
we limit our recognition of WHO we are.

The mind is golden
but it, too
is lesser than spirit.

Our True Self is bigger
than the body-mind
can imagine.

We are not a body
with a mind and spirit inside.

We are a spirit
using a body and mind
to experience, play, and learn from
a Journey in the Earth Dream Theater
as an integrated body-mind-spirit.

We are the Universe
in full awareness of itself,
joyfully dancing the Spiral
and Singing the Songs.

aaheart+++

The most well-known among the Copenhagen interpretations of quantum physics that embrace a fundamental role for thought and consciousness is attributed to a trio of eminent physicists whose contributions were central to the field, John von Neumann, John Archibald Wheeler, and Eugene Wigner. They brought a premise that thought and consciousness are not just artifacts of the biochemical processes of the brain; rather, thought and consciousness are the fundamental causative factors of the cosmos. Thought and consciousness create matter.[POG 125-6]

God is the life-dreamer who is becoming Conscious through Creation.[LJ 199] As it happens, Science and Gnosticism are natural allies, mutually supportive co-authors of unfolding the mystery of Life, God, and Consciousness. We are co-creators participating in this evolving of Consciousness, one with the Creator and the Creation.[LJ 197]

But, thoughts don't exist in the world. They are not things. They are not made of matter... So? What if awareness is the basis for reality instead of matter? If awareness was the basis of reality, then everything else exists as an experience within awareness. Matter would exist because of awareness. Science has discovered that solid matter is actually mostly empty space and some weird quantum particles whizzing around, and if it were not for an intelligent observer even that would not exist.[LJ 190]

Quantum physics has shown that Intelligent consciousness is the director and producer of the cosmic movie.[OG 130] Science and religion find common ground in consciousness. Max Planck, winner of a Nobel Prize has declared that "I regard consciousness as fundamental. I regard matter as a derivative of consciousness... Everything that we talk about, that we regard as existing, [suggests] consciousness."

Quantum physicists found that in experimenting on the nature of matter, the matter-wave would not show up as matter without an 'intelligent' observer. Later, as scientists tried to understand the theory that became the basis for the Holographic universe, they came to understand that our observation of the hologram made the universe show up as matter. This provides an opening to suggest that the WHO we are is part of the process of creating the material universe from the hologram. Who we are is much more than what we are. Who we are is co-creators who were part of the original creation. We might choose to be born into a what, a body that can live in a 4-dimensional universe (3D+ time) and when that body dies, we remain conscious without that body, but continue our consciousness in a 2-dimensional world, as seen by millions of near-death experiencers.

Larry Dossey, MD writes, "My conclusion is that consciousness is not a thing or substance, but a non-local phenomenon. Non-local is a fancy word for infinite. If something is non-local, it is not localized to specific points in space… or to specific points in time. Non-local events are immediate; they require no travel time… they require no energetic signal to carry them… they do not become weaker with increasing distance, [they] are omnipresent, everywhere at once. This means there is no necessity for them to go anywhere; they are already there. They are infinite… present at all moments, past, present, and future, meaning they are eternal."—Science of Premonitions p.191

Infinite and eternal—sounds like attributes of God.

Sir James Jeans, physicist has declared: "… the universe begins to look more like a great thought than like a great machine. Mind no longer appears to be an accidental intruder into the realm of matter. Get over it and accept the inarguable conclusion. The universe is not material, mental and spiritual." [POG 129]

Michio Kaku, string theorist, concluded that we are in a world made by rules created by an Intelligence. To me it is clear we exist in a plan which is governed by rules that were created by a universal intelligence and not by chance. [POG 129]

The light-show illusion that is our physical universe is continuously and constantly created by a 2-dimensional energy-verse. It exists in a neighboring alternative 'brane-verse', inaccessible to us and invisible to us, but which can be affected by laws that inform the energy-verse's continuous creation of our physical universe which springs from infinite, nonlocal, Intelligent Consciousness. The screen play for the cosmic movie, the 2D holographic system that projects the cosmic movie, and the resulting light-show illusion creates the 3D cosmic movie—all originate from and are guided by Intelligent Consciousness —God! [POG 131]

The spirals whirled and sang.
"He has found the path he was seeking, he listened and discovered Wisdom," whispered a Grandmother.
"He knew the truth and the way but didn't realize that he was already there!" cried the Dreamkeeper. "He knew, he listened, he learned, he remembered!"
"Now he will show others the path to full consciousness and wisdom," beamed a Grandfather. "Life can be a dream, sweet heart. Hello. Hello again. Here's hoping we can meet again." The spirals all sang, "Sh-BOOM!"

WHO I AM Is More Than What I Seem To Be

My SELF Is WHO I AM.

My expression of WHO I AM
is what I 'seem' to be.

My SELF is the producer of Reality,
WHAT is the production of SELF.

Nothing is SELF-Originated
Everything is Originated
Sustained,
Completed and Disappeared in WHO.

WHO sustains WHAT.
WHAT is sustained by WHO.
WHO is the source,

WHAT appears to be,

changes,
and disappears.

WHO IS,
WHAT appears to be.

Without WHAT,
WHO IS.

Without WHO,
Nothing IS.

Before you were born,
WHO IS.

WHAT has beginning, so WHAT ends.

WHO is beginningless, so WHO never ends.

WHO perceives,
WHAT doesn't.

WHO sustains WHAT by WHO's perceiving.
WHAT by itself disappears.

WHO cares,
WHAT doesn't.

WHAT 'matters'
WHO doesn't.

WHAT is significant,

WHO grants significance.

WHAT intends,
WHO laughs.

WHAT is enjoyed,
WHO enjoys WHAT.

WHAT works,
WHO plays.

WHAT works within WHO's playing.
Outside of WHO's playing, nothing works.
WHAT is WHO's field of play.

WHO is WHAT's mover.
WHAT is moved by WHO.

WHO expresses through WHAT,
WHAT is WHO's expression.

Nothing is WHO's silence.
WHAT and nothing are WHO's binary code of 1s and 0s,
the two corners of WHO's smile.
For WHO these two are the same.

When WHO's identified with WHAT,
seriousness and suffering arise.

When WHO's identified with nothing,
Humor and freedom arise as so much loose change.

* * *

As a changing WHAT trying
to grab a 'stable' changing WHAT,
even change is changing.

WHAT changes,
WHO doesn't.

WHAT has problems.
WHO has problems, and no problems,

1s and 0s of binary code.
WHO holds both the same way and laughs.

Existence is a lark.

You as WHO is relation beyond all things,
and nowhere, beyond time and space.

You as WHAT
are at the effect of whatever, everywhere.

WHAT you are is birth and death without end.
WHO you are is beyond all limitation.

WHAT you are agonizes about its ever-ceasing to be.
WHO you are joyfully plays in WHAT's ever-becoming.

When WHAT's ever-becoming cancels WHAT's ever-
ceasing to be
WHO smiles.

WHAT matters to WHO.

WHO is invisible to WHAT.

WHAT is the 'matter' with WHO.
Without WHO, WHAT doesn't 'matter.'

Without WHAT,
WHO is the same.

With WHAT, WHO is the same
and different,
in two different worlds.
quantum world and world of time and space.

For WHAT, the same is difference.
For WHO the differences are the same.

Existence is 1s and 0s.
WHAT is 1 or isn't.
WHO is one, many, and isn't.

WHAT is he, she, it, them—objects.
WHO is YOU, WE, US—

WHO expresses WHAT
and knows it.

WHAT is expressed
and knows not.

Together WE ARE.
Separated what can be.

* * *

I AM WHO WE ARE.
WE ARE WHO I AM
WE ARE WHO WE ARE.
I AM WHO I AM.

WHAT stands between us.
WHO knows,
WHAT doesn't.

Knowing that,
we hold no position 'between.'

WHAT has beginning
So, WHAT ends.

Who is beginningless,
So, WHO never ends.

Knowing this you can live in freedom and joy.
With courage, let go of the WHAT
To live as though your WHAT is simply an expression
Of WHO You Are.

Live playfully here and now knowing that WHAT is
WHO's field of play.
All there is, is… Ex-IS-tence!

BE!

aaheart+++

It's valuable to know this, that you existed before you were born, and you will continue to exist in consciousness no matter what happens in the coming cataclysm. This is your ticket to ride free of fears or worry. When you wake up and live as though you know WHO you are, you are already in Heaven, here on Earth—Gospel of Thomas. You are awareness experiencing the NOW moment, a witness of experience, being,[IJ 135] as awareness and the world exists in You.[IJ 137]

Does Gnosis make you immortal? Gnosis is becoming conscious that, as consciousness, you are already immortal and always have been. Time exists in you. You are awareness watching the appearances flow by.[IJ 137]

This is the fundamental discovery of the Gnostics, the original Christians, who discovered not to identify with the (WHAT) experience, instead identifying with the experiencer. This state of contemplation is getting back to the primal simplicity of being the conscious witness (WHO) of the unfolding events that create the drama of our lives. We can watch *Days Of Our Lives* without thinking we are real people in this soap opera that has our name listed in the credits as one of the actors. We are not living our lives on the psyche-body (WHAT), thoughts and actions arise within this experience, and we just enjoy the show knowing (gnosis) that WHO we are is at play in WHAT. Gnosis is a way of 'travelling', not a destination. The more we wake up, the more we love living.[IJ 147]

The downside of believing you are the body, is the inevitability of death. But WHO you are existed before your body was birthed. WHO is beginningless, so WHO does not die. WHAT had a beginning so what gets whacked. Capiche? Fear of death is often what motivates spiritual exploration. The personal search for deeper understanding is a quest for a deeper identity which can survive death. As we complete this process, we realize we are Consciousness itself. Consciousness (WHO) was never born, and so only WHAT, which was born, will die. WHO is eternal.

In the world language used by the original Christians, the word usually translated as 'salvation' also means 'preservation'. 'To be saved' is 'to be preserved', or 'made permanent'. When we realize we are the permanent presence of Consciousness (WHO), not the temporary ever-changing psyche-body (WHAT), we know we are safe at home, the game-winning score! We know something of the reality of this from the testimony of near-death experiences.

Eventually, we learn to stand right back inside our WHAT costume and be the incredibly awesome watcher of our experience. The WHO reality becomes the quite dramatic experience we are watching. We watch from the cheap seats in the balcony, engrossed in the drama, but existing outside of it as the invulnerable and immortal WHO. We realize the Knowledge, the Gnosis, becoming aware of the dazzling darkness of the Mystery. We immerse ourselves each night in this wonderful absence of experience in the state of deep sleep, a stillness without movement, the ground of all experience. We aren't aware of it because it is not an experience. When we focus on the permanent presence that witnesses our ever-changing experience, we become conscious of Consciousness. We can let go of our concept of reality and live in the Mystery, allowing life to continually surprise us with its infinite innovations and dramatic rodeos.

The Son is the Consciousness of the Father, the Father is the Mystery—the dazzling darkness of unconscious Consciousness. Christian master, Marcus has Jesus saying: "I am the Son of the Father who is beyond all existence.

While I, his Son, is in existence." Resurrection represents spiritual awakening. The original Christians taught that we each need to resurrect, which means to awaken from the illusion, and we need to wake up to our true WHO identity.

Gnosis is knowing we DON'T know, a surrender of knowing nothing and loving all, everything. In that reality shift we discover we are more than we ever imagined, or ever could imagine. Gnosis is understanding that we are utterly safe because the illusion of our existence is outside the human predicament completely. We realize Gnosis when we become aware that we knew the answer in the first place. We began searching for meaning because life didn't make sense—and we were right! Life DOESN'T make sense! It's an absolute mystery!

Both Science and Gnosticism are based on questioning WHAT is taken for granted. Both refuse to accept any analysis on blind faith. Science is trying to understand something so complex that it can't be comprehended. Gnosticism is trying to understand something so simple it can't be comprehended.

Our WHAT comes and goes within awareness every day when we arise in the morning and disappears when we sleep at night. You can see yourself as WHO you really are —an unborn and undying awareness witnessing a flow of experiences which had no beginning and will never end, within which you will always appear to be an individual part of Consciousness in relationship with the whole."[IJ 149]

The Gnostic knows that the person we appear to be, the life-dreamer (WHAT) is not WHO we truly are, the Consciousness that plays the role of WHAT in the life dream. Everything in the life-dream ends because WHAT has a beginning, but as awareness WHO is beginningless, so WHO is eternal and will never die. Death is by its nature a profound mystery, and one of the tasks it plays in life is to remind us of the mystery which is ever-present in each moment."[IJ 147]

Gnosis does not make you immortal. Gnosis is becoming conscious that you (WHO) are already immortal and always have been."[IJ 137] We mimic Gnosis when we play a video game and (WHAT) dies, WHO gets beer from the fridge and has chips and guacamole. Lucid living is being conscious that you have two separate aspects to your identity right now. Your apparent nature (WHAT) is the person you appear to be in the life-dream, but your essential nature (WHO) is awareness that turns the video game on to play the game to experience the drama of the make-believe life-dream."[IJ 137]

Many Dreams

All dreams,
large and small,
even those you judge to be bad,
lead you to your True Nature.

Your many dreams
dance and play
in the gardens
of the spirit world,
beyond and within the illusion
that we call Reality.

aaheart+++

Life is one awareness becoming conscious of itself in infinitely various forms."[IJ 213-4]

* * *

A human being is a part of a whole, called by us the 'universe', a part limited in time and space. He experiences himself, his thoughts and feelings, as something separated from the rest—a kind of optical delusion of his consciousness. This delusion is a kind of prison for us, restricting us to our personal desires and to affection for a few persons nearest to us. Our task must be to free ourselves from this prison by widening our circle of compassion to embrace all living creatures and the whole of nature in its beauty.—Albert Einstein

The good news is we are all one—the bad news is: only a small minority of us realizes this.[LJ 206] We need to obey "the law inscribed on the heart", as Valentinus put it.[LJ 203] Gnostics view God as the life-dreamer WHO is becoming conscious through creation.[LJ 199]

"Knowing God IS eternal life."—John 17:3.

Eternity is now, not just later. Gnosis IS eternity. There is no separate you to be free, or otherwise. There is only You, the life-dreamer, dreaming the life-dream.[LJ 173] Gnostics compare life to a dream and gnosis to waking up, because you will feel as if you have awakened from some sort of unconscious stupor. You will have begun to rouse yourself from the collective coma we mistake for 'real life' by becoming conscious of reality itself.[LJ 132]

"One moment of a man's life is a fact so stupendous as to take the lustre out of all fiction."—Ralph Waldo Emerson

Those WHO have experienced heaven and lived to tell about it describe it as an experience of unconditional love. The realities of realities, the incomprehensibly glorious truth of truths that lives and breathes at the core of everything that exists or ever will exist… not only the most important emotional truth in the universe, but also the single most important scientific truth as well.[POH 71]

The spirals celebrated with gentle song and dance.
"He remembers the way of the word,
Remembers the songs he has heard,
With a heart full of love and his soul in tune,
A white fiery sun and placid moon.
He is one in the loving, cosmic heart of all.
We spiral around,
Around and around,
The Heartbeat of the Earth."

Meditation Basics

For more than 35 years, Bagwhan Shree Rajneesh studied, practiced and demonstrated elements of the traditions of many of the world's great religious, mystical and esoteric traditions. His talks on his discoveries are published in 350 books in English, and many more in Chinese, Danish, Dutch, Finnish, French, German, Greek, Hebrew, Italian, Japanese, Korean, Polish, Portuguese, Russian, Serbo-Croat, Spanish, and Swedish. I don't remember ever taking a course from anybody or even reading about it, but somehow I did seem to have meditated some time along my journey without knowing about it... sort of a natural form of meditation, a way to meditate that anyone could practice and use.

As I think way back to my childhood, I had a lot of time on my own with a huge world to explore, a larger world to imagine, and an even larger world to create, sometimes with my younger brother, but mostly alone.

Rajneesh summed up the bare essentials in his book *Meditation: The First and Last Freedom*. Baghwan has said, "Meditation is not something new; you have come with it into the world. Mind is something new, meditation is your nature. It is your very being. How can it be difficult?"

Ok, I was born with it. Meditation came with me into this world so it was one of my first toys, and I used this toy with trees and barns and outhouses, all of which were full of wonder, especially when I climbed to their tops to see the world from a new and wonderful vantage point. Later in life, this childhood exploration would pay dividends when I happened to meet the young proprietor of Deepwoods Apothecary Shoppe in Arlington, Texas, to whom I was showing my dreamcatchers of the Seventh Fire Dreamcatcher Heritage Collection. When I mentioned I had seen my first dreamcatcher at a museum on the Mille Lacs Indian Reservation in Minnesota, her eyes lit up, her mouth dropped open, and she told me of a lucid vision she had experienced only a few weeks ago as though through the eyes of a male, in the 1950's from the top of a barn in Minnesota looking out over the farms of the countryside.

She would not have been born when that happened to me, thirty some years later, and hundreds of miles away! That mystery would later initiate the writing of my first book, *Dancing a Quantum Dream*, to sort out the many strange experiences I'd pushed aside in the business of living. I was free to experience.

Clearly, I was a dreamer back then. In 5th grade I was cluttering my math assignments with artwork, stories and poetry. Mrs. Butts let me explore on my own. In 6th grade, while everyone else was chip-carving pine boxes and plates to be given to our mothers on Mother's Day, I chose to work on an image of a quiet cabin perched on a promontory among forests and mountains that I'd seen as a shadow on my bedroom door. I was drawn to that secluded mountain apparition to refine and clarify its significance to my childhood experience. To her credit, Miss Esping didn't require me to follow the rest of the class and allowed my own voyage of discovery, wherever it would lead me.

In 7th grade I had access to everything in the High School Library from *Miss Pickerel Goes to Mars* to *Les Misérables* and the *Collected Works of A. Conan Doyle*. I read over 70 books that year. That kept my very active imagination busy. Then I discovered the County Library near downtown Waseca, the County seat where my Mom and Dad went shopping every Saturday. They'd drop me off and I'd nearly have the library to myself to roam the stacks of books and bring some home, along with the few Sci-Fi books I'd buy cheap at the bookstore. *Worlds in Collision*, *Earth in Upheaval* and *Ages in Chaos*, all by Immanuel Velikovsky, held my rapt attention for hours at a time.

I kept getting in trouble with rules, regulations, and opprobrium, like most teens, I suppose. Jumping out a 1st floor window to join classmates on the playground seemed ok to me, but not to my teacher. Then one exciting basketball game that would decide a championship, I left my seat in the bleachers to go to the restroom and on my return, the game was close and nearing its exciting end, so I chose to watch the last few minutes from a crowded lane next to the bleachers. The superintendent of schools ordered me to sit in the bleachers. My seat was no longer available, so he ordered me to sit on the steps. I objected because I didn't want to sit on the dirty steps. He angrily grabbed my shirt and repeated his order. I couldn't help but notice his hands were shaking, and I made that an oral observation. He dragged me out to a hallway where he released me to fall on the hard terrazzo floor. I instinctively grabbed for whatever my hands could find to avoid injury—I found his shirt and ripped all the buttons off as I thudded to the floor. I was expelled for a week and my Dad had to meet him to get me back in school.

Maybe I was just a free-thinker, and all things were possible to my mind, now called neuroplasticity.

Far from being fixed from birth, the brain is easily the most changeable organ in the body. The most effective tool for rewiring the brain for subtle perception, is meditation. Meditation enables us to slow and eventually stop the automatic firing of our neural fireworks show, that leaves us dazzled and distracted by the familiar world, and unable to establish another higher level of perception.

Relaxed concentration at a point between our eyebrows activates the prefrontal cortex which can switch off the circuits in the rest of the brain so we can perceive the subtle, nonlocal realities beyond sensory awareness—the thrill of the life force moving in the core of our being, our heart doing what it always does if the brain does not overrule its freedom—feelings of peace, love, harmony, and joy. We may see light or have inspiring insights… just for openers.[POG 150-1]

This is the experience of God, or just as meaningfully, the experience of our Self or Soul. Because we are in essence, godlike, one with God, the experience is not reserved for cloistered monks or nuns, or yogis in remote Himalayan monasteries or caves. Anyone, anywhere who achieves stillness and complete inner absorption shares the same universal experience, even a farm kid from Minnesota.

Regular practice of meditation by repetition forms new neural pathways. With supportive circuits formed to support it, it becomes increasingly easy to meditate. I suspect that monotonous, long hours of sitting on the tractor with little else to do, I was able to begin meditation 101 without formal instruction. I just fell into a practice of meditation on a tractor with a beautiful sky above and the wind and clouds to allow me to fall into a meditative state naturally, or agriculturally, as it were. The nights meditating on the moon and stars, the aurora borealis, fishing, milking, gathering eggs, hooking rogue corn plants out of acres of soybeans, walking two miles by country roads to school in

1st, 2nd, 3rd, 4th grades, climbing to the peak of the barn roof to gaze upon the vast countryside, gathering gooseberries in the woods, an idyllic paradise upon which to quietly meditate. I was always bringing school assignments home after school—and leaving them on Mom's ironing board in the kitchen to take back to school the next day.

Yet, I graduated at the head of my class, on the Honor's list at college, and graduated Summa Cum Laude. I earned an MA while coaching colleagues in prep for their comps. I discovered intuitive energy healing, intuited Gnostic poetry half a century before I knew what Gnosticism was, meditated 2-3 minutes to enter the afterlife to communicate with an acquaintance's deceased husband, intuited how to weave dreamcatchers and the deep spiritual wisdom teachings that accompanied them, then intuit the Gnostic Now moments, and write and illustrate a children's book, *The Dance of the Quantum Acorn*. With no instruction, I fell into a deep meditation one evening that brought me to the dazzling darkness of the Gnostics, the presence of God—and I didn't even fall off the tractor.

Lest transcendence seems too high a mountain to climb, the good news for those who, like me, have yet to master perfect stillness and complete inner absorption, is that meditation brings many benefits long before full transcendence is achieved.

Wow! What might I achieve if I made a consistent practice of what I merely intuited without a template to follow. If you practice meditation to perfection, attaining perfect stillness and inner absorption, you can experience oneness with God. This is the essential teaching of all religions and the message of all the saints, sages, and saviors who ever lived.[POG 158-9]

"Behold, you have the kingdom of God within you."—Luke 17:21

This intimate connection between the human observers and the Universe is possibly a rarely observed reality. I remember walking alone one night in a quiet suburban neighborhood when suddenly a streetlight above me crackled and went dark. Odd, I thought. I walked toward a better lit area further along the street and that next streetlight also crackled and went dark. Wow... very odd! Then a porch light to my left went poof and went dark... OK, this is bordering on spooky. That night, eight lights near me suddenly went dark as I approached. I just laughed it off, and forgot about it... of course!

Just a shaman in plain clothes doing quiet miracles. I didn't have to put fingers together in a certain way, or cross my legs just so, close my eyes or moan **ommm** monotonously. I'd just get off the tractor and walk over to the creek, clear a spot to lie on my back and just let the clouds play. At night, I'd take a beach towel and a pillow out on the front lawn and lay there to look up at the stars, or the northern lights, smile and wave as a meteor flashed by—always abiding peacefully in the Now Moment. When I ate, I would simply eat. Walking to school, I'd just walk, not thinking about getting there. I eventually invented a little beep-beep game as I shuffled along with my brother to keep our mind from wandering, just keeping a steady pace. Beep-beep and I'd shuffle faster to pass him, then he'd do the same so our attention was fully on walking while having a little fun. That's what meditation is, just remain in the Now Moment in whatever you are doing.

Similarly, when out in the fields hooking corn out of the bean rows, under a broad beautiful sky, just trudging along one Now Moment after another.

Dr. Paul Pearsall suggests that cardio-contemplation is similar in some ways to meditation, but unique in its focus on the heart. It is a merging, collective, and connective process that allows us to tune into the memory of what it feels like to adore being alive.[THC 153] Virtually every spiritual and religious tradition includes some form of meditation. Research shows that meditative states affect healthy physical changes throughout the body, such as slower, deeper breathing, reduced heart rate, and lowered blood pressure. Concentration meditations focus attention or awareness on one's breath, a word (mantra), or religious phrase mentally repeated as one breathes deeply. Opening-up techniques involve awareness of the Now Moment, free of judgment, allowing any distracting thoughts to simply pass as clouds across the sky, as Baghwan Shree Rajneesh describes. Spencer Holst calls it 'brilliant silence', letting our heart be open to its natural resonation with all the energies of the Now Moment and allowing those experiences to disappear as we are immersed completely in the now moment, the present quantum moment.[THC 153-155]

Ultimately, the key to mastery of meditation is witnessing the Now Moment. Baghwan would just remind us, "Witnessing simply means a detached witnessing, an unprejudiced Now Moment—that's the whole secret of meditation! Nothing needs to be done, just be a witness, an observer, a watcher, looking at the traffic of the mind, thoughts just passing by, desires, memories, dreams, fantasies. Simply stand at the side of the road watching the parade going by, aloof, calm, just watching it with no judgement, no condemnation, Not saying, 'this is good' or 'this is bad.' It just IS!"

Your inner being is
Nothing but the inner sky.

Clouds come and go.

Planets are born and disappear.

Stars rise
Stars set.

The Inner sky
Remains cloudless.
Always the same—
Untouched, untarnished, endless.

That inner sky we call the witness.
That is the whole plan of meditation.
Go in, enjoy the inner sky.

Remember, whatsoever you can see—
You are not that.

You can see thoughts,
Then you are not thoughts.
You can see your feelings,
you are not your feelings.

You can see your dreams,
desires, memories, imaginations, projections,
but you are not them.

Go on eliminating all that you can see.
Then one day the sky will be clear.

A most significant moment in your life.
All that was seen has disappeared and
only the seer is there.

***

The seer is the empty sky.
To know it is to be filled with love.
To know it is to be one with God
And immortal.

There is only one sky.

—Bagwan Shree Rajneesh in Meditation: The First and Last Freedom p. xvi

Experiment playfully. Use music if you like. Witnessing is like growing seeds. Go to nature. Life is a game. As children, we rarely have difficulty enjoying Life. The toddler might giggle, laugh or scream with joy at the thrill that is life. It just bubbles over. Then it sometimes gets a bit grim and sometimes that cloud darkens much or all our lives, so it no longer feels like much fun at all. Gnosticism is an attempt to change the way we look at life to rediscover that joy we once might have felt nearly all the time. The experience of life hasn't changed—we have changed. We have changed the way we looked at life. Gnosticism is a new way to play that game so we can once again rediscover that freedom to laugh and love and even bubble with mirth and joy. That's because a gnostic knows he existed before he was born, and he will always exist because he knows his consciousness is eternal. He is One with God and Heaven is his home. The purpose of this 3D sojourn in this earthly life is to explore the full possibilities of consciousness.

Meditation is a very ancient, basic and effective means of going inwards to train your mind to reach a new state of consciousness. We can listen to the sissagwad, the gentle spirit wind in the trees to enter an ecstatic state of trance to access other worlds that might hold unexpected wisdoms useful to survival. Grandmother and Grandfather spirits whisper wisdom if we learn to listen.

We must learn how to create our own vision and intuition to create our own rituals and ceremonies. Ecstatic experiences can increase your capacity to function at levels far beyond what you can imagine. This book is a guide to an authentic path that resonates within the cultural context of your existing society. Drumming can be a path that can help you realign with the natural pulse of Earth and Sun. Drumming can be a way to quiet the noise of our monkey-chattering mind so we can hear the sound of the apocalyptic train on the cosmic tracks.[SD 77] You might also discover a more beautiful world than you could imagine.

Meditation is little more than training your mind to become more self-aware and more aware of your world. Meditation is a learned skill to train your mind to function at its peak capacity, and like any workout, the more you exercise it the better it works. If everybody knew how good meditation makes them feel, everybody would do it. Here is one of many meditation techniques:[POG 177]

> Choose an upright sitting position that allows you to sit comfortably in a quiet space that will not be disturbed, not too warm, perhaps a bit on the cool side with adequate ventilation, and loose fitting clothing. A chair has been the preference of deep meditators who have done this for many years, although some like a kneeling bench, or a kneeling pillow, sit cross-legged or not.
>
> If you choose to sit, keep your spine straight and upright without leaning back and your feet should be flat on the floor. Your thighs should be parallel to the floor. Short people might use a cushion or pillow under their feet. Tall people might need to sit on a pillow to get the right

position. If this causes back stress go ahead and use a pillow but try to maintain the straight spine without leaning back on the pillow. Keep your head level, eyes forward. Relax your shoulders and rest your hands loosely in your lap, palms up, little fingers against your tummy, to help you hold this position comfortably.[POG 178]

Once you are seated comfortably, two short breathing exercises will help relax and settle your body. While inhaling sharply through your nose and then a long, slow deep inhalation, tense your whole body and hold your breath for a few seconds. Then take one sharp, then a second deep exhale as you count silently to eight. Without a pause, inhale again to a silent count of eight, then exhale through your mouth with one long exhalation, releasing all tension in your body, Repeat this 3 to 6 times.

Next, inhale slowly as you count silently to eight, hold for eight counts, then exhale for a silent count of eight. Without pausing, inhale deeply again to a silent count of eight, hold for a silent count of eight, and exhale slowly to a silent count of eight. Repeat 3-6 times. You can vary the count to adjust to your lung capacity but keep inhalation, hold, and exhalation the same. Finish your breathing practice by inhaling deeply and then completely exhaling. Now you are ready to begin **Hong Sau** meditation.[POG 179]

Eyes closed, wait for your next breath to come in naturally. When that first breath enters, think HONG (rhymes with 'song.') Don't hold your breath. When you exhale naturally, think SAU (rhymes with 'saw'). This is an ancient mantra that means, **I am He** or **I am spirit**.[POG 180]

Make no attempt to control your breath now. Just observe it flowing in and out at first. Then, as your breathing calms down, focus your attention on the coolness as you breathe in and the warmth as you breathe out. Eventually you may become aware of the coolness of your inhalation deeper in your nose and the warmth there when you breathe out warmed air. And then the cool and warm on the point between your eyebrows. Keeping your eyes closed and relaxed bring you focus there. No strain or crossed eyes. Mostly at first it will be a gentle attention as if looking at a distant point as you notice the cool and warm of the breath on that point between your eyebrows.

If your mind wanders just bring it back to your awareness and your repeating HONG SAU silently. You're training your mind, so be gentle and forgiving with yourself, but vigilant and insistent. Enjoy Hong Sau at least once a day for 15 minutes. Later, you can extend this to 30 minutes, then to an hour or more. Reserve some time after meditation to just quietly abide in the effects of the meditation. Eventually you can meditate morning and evening. It often will seem that you have difficulty maintaining the focus on your breathing and on silently repeating the Hong Sau mantra in rhythm with your breathing, or judge yourself not capable of meditation. Everybody breathes as long as they live. This meditation is not a business, it's a simple skill that you can learn, like any other. Just be patient with yourself. Your concentration will improve. Remember, you are just breathing naturally, not pushing air in and out.[POG 181]

If this keeps happening when you meditate, return to the preparatory exercises using double the times, 6-12 minutes, instead of 3-6.[POG 182] If your breathing become shallow or the rhythm slows and inhalation gets deeper, that's good! Your heartbeat may also slow down. When demand for oxygen calls for heartbeat or more breathing, your body will respond to get what you need. Soon, you may see different colors of light in the darkness of your closed eyes. It might be white, blue or golden, or all three. The light might take the form of a circle, often a deep azure blue field surrounded by a golden light, with a tiny white star in the center—usually called the 'spiritual eye.'

"If therefore thine eye be single, thine whole body shall be full of light."—Matthew 6:22

You might get the experience, 'the peace that passes all understanding.' When you get there, you will know what millions have come to know, that there is another world within you and that you are experiencing your Self in God.

Moving toward Lucid Living you can:

1. Use your breathing meditation as your foundation for awakening. Or, even if you are walking under a beautiful sky, or in a garden, a forest, along a seashore, or in a majestic grove of redwood or sequoia—just begin to remind yourself that you are asleep and now you are ready to awaken. Remember, awakening is a relative state. If you feel you have awakened, allow yourself to awaken still more.
2. Second step is to practice disconnecting from the person you seem to be to become a witness to all that you are experiencing. WHO you are is experiencing through WHAT.
3. Embrace everything with full acceptance and compassion to be one with ALL—BIG LOVE.
4. Putting it all together, stay conscious of that oneness, unconditionally aware, appreciating life as it is—an open-ended, collective experience of this life-dream, giving and getting the most from the life dream you share.

Another everyday practice you can use is breathing in—be consciously awareness of everyone and everything—

Allness. Breathing out, send loving breath that embraces our Oneness. Just replace Hong-Saw with the thought—Allness/Oneness.[IJ 221-223]

Just sitting and breathing, witness whatever you are feeling, hearing, seeing and smelling. Those experiences exist within awareness. Now witness your thoughts coming and going. WHO you are is not the thinker. WHO you are is witnessing what you are, a human being doing thinking. If you get caught up in your thoughts, just start over, no harm done, it's part of the practice. If you find the deep relaxation pleasurable, enjoy it, but recall that you are witnessing. It's almost as though WHO you are is practically spying on the experience of WHAT perceiving. That's not a violation of WHAT's privacy though, because that's just how it's set up. WHO you are is awareness that is witnessing a flow of appearances of the life and times of what you are. The Awakening is resurrection. It's the same word in Greek.

Remember, WHO you are is one with consciousness and eternity, a co-creator; whereas what you are is a three-dimensional being experiencing a life in a three-dimensional creation. WHAT dies—WHO doesn't. The world is an illusion, a hologram. It appears to exist with the presence of Consciousness. When we awaken to the way things are really set up, we realize death is safe. So is life. Fearing and struggling against death is like a young child fearing and resisting sleep. Yet when the body is renewed by rest, we wake up. It's like looking in a mirror: we don't fear looking away from the mirror. When we stop watching or blink, does the reflection die? No, of course not. So it is with sleeping. When you are sleeping, WHO you are doesn't die. WHAT is merely recovering from the work of maintaining brain activity for so long and needs to recharge, because it's a 3D being, like an electric car recharging. Not to worry, it will move when you turn the key tomorrow. Death is the proof that WHO we are is not attached to the 3D person, what we seem to be. And we don't need to fear life any more than we need to fear a dream. Death is an opportunity for our consciousness to merge with the 'dazzling darkness,' the presence of God.[LJ 163-165]

The more we identify with our WHAT, the more frightened of life we become. The more we are aware we are NOT that, that we are a conscious, silent observer, the more we free ourselves to fully engage with the dramas of the soap operas of life, while WHO participates from the balcony, the cheap seats. It doesn't mean we have to be perfect, but that we accept living life fully, which means we are continually offered opportunities we need to wake up and become more conscious.

The spirals danced and whirled as though they really loved the dance.
"He has got it together since childhood and as an adult!" they sang as one.
"He had to put it together mostly from his life experiences and very little outside help," roared the Dreamkeeper, "except he left quite a set of stage directions. Kept everyone busy setting it all in place so that it would unfold as naturally as possible."
"That was a nice touch to include his family in the drama. They performed almost perfectly without having a script," sighed a Grandmother.
The spirals danced a spiral.

Meditation Through The Hearts Code

As an undergraduate at Cornell, studying electrical engineering and pre-medicine, Dr. Gary Schwarz took courses in classical and quantum physics. He saw that quantum physics demonstrated "in no uncertain terms, that everything is, in fact, uncertain... sub-atomic systems like photons and electrons exist more like distributed waves or fuzzy clouds than discrete objects or particles; that is until they're observed or measured... they are, relatively speaking, here, and there, and everywhere to various degrees, waiting to 'materialize' in a specific form. Quantum phenomena are weird, to say the least." [LEU 24]

To Einstein's formula we can add 'Information' as another aspect comparable to 'Energy.' [HC 51] Albert Einstein was a hero to Dr. Schwarz. He had been taught that Einstein conceived $E=MC^2$, his famous formula while taking an imaginary ride on a light beam, looking at the universe around him. What he saw when he became one with the light beam, gave him a new vision that forever changed how we all now see the universe.

Dr. Schwarz emulated Einstein by imagining riding an electron in a system from point A to point B and back again. He took that ride again and again before describing it simply, non-mathematically. A to B back to A, what returned to A was the history of A as interpreted by B and returned to A in revised form. This systemic memory process forms the basis of universal living memory.[LEU 25]

Not only does a system hold a memory of the past, but the past is interpreted and revised to be integrated with the present. Scientists study living feedback systems using this formula.[LEU 26] This can be applied to spirituality as well as science, and sociology as well as theology.[LEU 28]

Heisenberg's Uncertainty Principle is a quantum fact of life that asserts that if we choose to measure one quantity, we inevitably alter the system and therefore cannot be certain of other quantities.[HC 46]

Cardio-contemplation allows one to become immersed in the quantum NOW moment, a brilliant silence and peak heart-awareness. Cardio-contemplation might be seen as one of the ways to connect with what some psychologists, most notably Carl Jung, called the collective unconscious. On some subtle energetic level, all the information gathered by those who have gone before us may still be represented in the memory system of every cell of our body. Being willing to be less cerebrally vigilant and more alert to subtle info-energy being resonated with every beat of the heart, may be similar to tuning a radio to a station that contains our collective cellular memory program. Cardio-contemplation may be a process that allows us to make contact with our soul by tapping into its spiritual energy. It may be one way to find our way back to the way things were supposed to be rather than yielding to the demands the brain's world constantly seems to be placing upon us. It may be a way to learn, communicate, and connect the physical experience of one's personality to knowledge contained within the vibrational structure of our shared consciousness—brain/heart/body Mind.[THC 153]

Cardio-contemplation is similar in some ways to meditation, but unique in its focus on the heart. It is a merging, collective, and connective process that allows us to tune into the memory of what it feels like to adore being alive… any of us might be able to allow free rein for our own hidden observer, that part of us that is alert and responsive to the thrill of living, even when the brain itself is busy and distracted trying to help us make a living.

Unaware of what I was doing as a young teen, I'd stop the tractor when I was out of sight of the farmstead and walk down to the little creek that flowed through the back forty, to lie on my back in the tall grass on the bank and watch the clouds play in the sky, and listen to the babbling of the little brook. Not very long, but more than ten minutes, closer to half an hour. And while I was plowing, disking or cultivating, I was singing, enjoying the beauty of a pleasant summer day, or just daydreaming, although I had to attend to minor annoyances such as steering the tractor —easy peasy. Sometimes, meditative moments were fleeting, but I took what I could and still got the job done. I had a panorama sky always. I even read with one eye on the furrow and one hand on the steering wheel. I discovered how to plow using the wide front of our Farmall M to gently hold one wheel up against the edge of the furrow so I could drive by Braille. I read *Grapes of Wrath* and other great books while driving that tractor.

After my parents' weekly grocery trip to town (and my visit to the county library) I'd read Immanuel Velikovsky's books on Earth catastrophes, as well as Bradbury's *Martian Chronicles* and *The Illustrated Man*, Asimov's *The Red Planet, Mars*, books by Arthur C. Clarke, Clifford Simak, Robert

Heinlein, John Steinbeck, Ernest Hemingway, and others. By that time, I had already read the Bible. I maintained a deep love for nature and science, lying on the lawn many nights contemplating the stars and the moon.

My friends were interested in meditation and one night I was invited to an 11:11 Convergence Celebration. After a few minutes of meditation, we were asked to share our meditations. All I could share was just 'brilliant blackness'. No one knew what that meant, but I finally discovered what it meant half a century later doing research on Gnosticism. Gregory of Nyssa and Dionysius called it the dazzling darkness—the one Consciousness of God. I was not able to see the light of God because I was essentially sitting in the lap of God and the light of God was shining past me, illuminating the darkness.[JALG 65] I had no idea! My catechism did not cover such things.

As I wrote earlier, I want this to be in your spiritual toolkit. Even better, I hope you will share this news as widely as you can to friends and family. It's just valuable to know that you existed before you were born, and you will continue to exist in consciousness no matter what happens in the coming cataclysm. Jesus wasn't kidding when he said his kingdom is not of this world—his kingdom is not the world of time and space, it's the world beyond time and space, a world of eternity and infinity.

Cardio-contemplation is not just time management or energy down-shifting. It is letting your heart open to its natural resonation with all the energies of the NOW moment. It thereby expands, or spiritually pauses, to allow energetics of oneself to completely immerse in the NOW moment, a quantum moment. In cardio-contemplation, you tune into the delicate info-energetic sensations that come from the heart rather than a word, sound, breathing, or image that can be experienced as coming from the consciousness somewhere in the brain. Mindfulness can stand in the way of thus enrolling the heart. That has a different purpose. Cardio-contemplation is a system for developing emotional awareness not by mental reflection, but by emotional focus on the energy center of the body—the heart. As the brain may be to intellectual intelligence, so the heart may be to emotional intelligence.[THC 155]

The process involves making a mental effort to shift focus to sensations coming from the heart instead of the head. Recalling a negative memory of the past, ask the heart for its insights on what might be a better way of dealing with the stressful situation. It would be helpful to monitor the heart with an electroencephalograph watching for smooth curves that indicate cardiac coherence.[THC 156]

Cardiac coherence, a blissful peaceful heart, enhances immunity and healing, freeing the natural healing instincts of the body to work their miracles.[THC 157]

Cardio-contemplation is NOT thinking about a new way to deal with stress. It's more like 'a talk to God so as not to bore Him', to allow the heart to fall into a state of resonance with the natural world and other hearts. Cellular memories become free to emerge so stress has less control over the brain/heart/body Mind.[THC 157]

> Beyond the Meadow of Light
> and the Forest Dark
> is a Garden of Pure Being.
>
> Open your heart
> and journey there with me,
> and we shall Dance the Spirals,
> and Sing the Songs
>
> aaheart+++

* * *

Learn—listen for your heart to tell you about living, loving, playing, and working joyfully.

> Country air soft with sunset and new-mown hay,
> makes each breath delicious
> and life more awesome.

Connect—send what you have learned to other hearts, the whole world around you.

> Under a golden summer sunny afternoon
> cloud-wisped, blue sky
> we raced raucously into the farmyard headlong,
> boysterously kicking dust into a storm around us.

aaheart+++

Philosopher Pierre Teilhard de Chardin wrote, "The ills from which we are suffering have had their seat in the very foundation of human thought." His words reflect the dangers of a world dominated by a heartless brain that seems to say, 'I am everything' while the often-ignored heart says 'I am nothing without everyone else.' Your brain may think it is on its own against the world, but your heart knows we are never truly alone.

Be Still. To tune into the heart, it's necessary to slow down and quiet down. That's all! Be still enough that you can become fully aware of the Now Moment instead of getting ready to launch into the Next Moment, or worrying about a messed up Past Moment. Remember what you learned about the Past? It's passed by, not here and now, no longer exists… nothing to be done about the past!

In the 13th century, Meister Eckhart reminded us "there is nothing in all creation so like God as stillness." Some people say, there's nothing as perfect as stillness—it's as simple as a deep breath and a deep sigh.

Lighten Up. Don't take yourself so seriously. Best advice from Godspell: "Ya gotta stay light to be the Light of the World." G.K. Chesterton wrote, "Angels fly because they take themselves lightly"… So, lighten up!

Shut Up. Stop talking, even to yourself. Quit gabbing to your self about the pleasure of eating or drinking, defending mental territory or abandoning territory, or seeking new territory, or seeking immediate physical pleasure. Practice ignoring the chattering monkey brain, have an inner conversation with that still inner observer, or turn over the job of taking care of everything for a bit to your inner observer to keep an eye on things for a bit. For a little while do just a bit less, say a little bit less.

Resonate. Cardio-contemplation is a form of receptive prayer, just listening to your heart.

Feel. Your heart is part of an info-energy system that can connect with other info-energy systems in the cosmos. You are not alone in the whole universe. You are connected to universal consciousness so don't cut yourself off from the All that you are. You are a Child of the Universe!

> "Through your eyes the stars can see!
> The brightness of a billion suns
> the cosmos knows through me."

Say that to yourself at least once a day and reflect on

what it means. You are one with all of creation which is aware of itself.

Be still, lighten up, shut up, resonate with your heart, feel, and listen for what your heart is telling you about living, loving, and working. Store that valuable feedback in every cell for later use in times of stress.

Connect. Broadcast your lessons silently received to the consciousness of the world around you and stay open to receive incoming energy from other awake hearts.[THC 158-159]

Heart-to-heart info-energetic connection is not just a theory. Research has shown that, by comparing electrocardiograms, one person's heartbeat can be measured in another person, particularly when they are touching. Holding hands in a prayer circle transcends the brain's illusion of control so that the created become One with the Creator, co-creators.[THC 164] Cardio-sensitivity, and connecting heart-to-heart requires receptivity, not judging and controlling, just accepting and welcoming connection.[THC 167]

The path to paradise and the gate of heaven is through the heart, and by having a warm open heart, we allow God's love to happen to us. If the heart acts like the soul's tuning fork, it may express the soul's code with every beat. The heart-to-heart connection operates in a higher range of frequency bands than the mind. A key part of falling in love is the experience of one's own heart falling into energetic resonance with another heart. The processes of connecting, nurturing, and integrating may explain why loving can feel like a sacred event representing the merging of two souls finally freed of obstacles to their energetic connection set up by their selfish, defensive brains.[THC 168-169]

Cardio-contemplation and the cardio-coherence that comes with it is one way to mend a broken or energy-disconnected heart.[THC 181]

When we are still enough to re-establish cardio-coherence, peaceful enough to love and be loved, and allow ourselves to suspend the brain's vigilance and arrogant prejudices, then we can become more aware of what our heart is telling us about another heart, and compassionate enough to be receptive to the subtle energy coming from that heart. That's when our brain can overcome its insensitivity to love. Without warning and beyond reason, the brain recognizes the much higher power than it can achieve in its constant search for dominance. Surrendering its need for control, the brain lets its heart join freely and without fear with another heart, and speaking from the heart, says, I love you.[THC 191]

T'ai Chi For The Heart

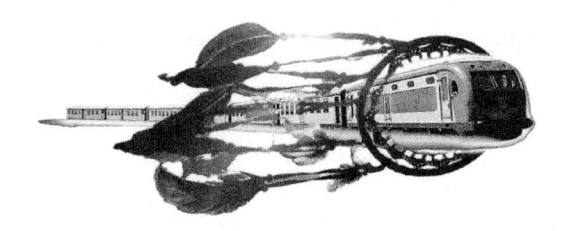

You are energy and everything around you is energy. Quantum energy is spiraling through time-space, into existence and out. Moving your body through this matrix of spiraling energy in a relaxed choreographed dance seems to induce a flow of energy in your whole body, much like an electric generator produces energy flow by cutting through lines of force. T'ai chi is a quantum dance as Justin Stone, originator of T'ai Chi Chih explains in his book.

The people of the crowded Orient know the feeling of serenity in the midst of activity. It is not by refraining from action that we achieve it, but by maintaining a firm, unchanging center in the midst of disturbance.

When we do the measured movements of T'ai Chi Chih, while focusing our concentration on the spot two inches below the navel, we feel the surge of Vital Force and experience a pleasant tingling. Yet, when we are quiet again, that center in the solar plexus is filled with power and we feel at rest. This serenity should spill over into our everyday lives, making possible a calm and joyous interior even in the most hectic times. [TCC]

My dear friend and partner Mary-Louise signed us up

for a T'ai Chi Chuan class at a senior center and then she discovered an easier form, T'ai Chi Chih, which was developed by a master teacher of T'ai Chi Chuan, Justin Stone. He found that students of the traditional form did not always fully experience the flow of chi energy, even after studying and practicing for several years. He returned to the original Qi Gong and Taoist manuscripts to reconstruct the traditional form into a more easily learned form he calls T'ai Chi for Serenity, T'ai Chi Chih.

We learned, and practiced T'ai Chi Chih and felt its power. Most people can learn and practice the twenty movements in about ten classes. The gentle, flowing movements promote health in every part of the body by circulating and balancing the Chi, the Vital Force. When our energies are out of balance, we might experience disease, distress, and disharmony. T'ai Chi does not require the adoption of any belief systems or chants. These are exercises all done with coordinated deep breathing in which inhalation is exaggerated by expanding belly as much as possible, hold for a count of three (about 3 seconds) and exhalation by flattening belly as much as possible, and hold for a count of three, (about 3 seconds.) This will bring a lot of healing oxygen to your body.

Exercises are not intended to punish, so do not feel you must push beyond your comfort zone. No need to do these exercises rapidly. Be gentle and loving toward yourself and enjoy the gentle movement. It's like a graceful dance with yourself and your inner being.

People have reported many physical, emotional, mental, and spiritual benefits of regular T'ai Chi practice. Daily practice brings about an increased awareness beyond self. It is a strong, vital path to transformation and wholeness and probably involves quantum energy.

Based on studies at Princeton's PEAR (Princeton

Engineering Anomalies Research) program and the experiences of his heart transplant patients, Pearsall recommends five basic principles involved in becoming aware of this mysterious quantum energy.

Be patient. Be connected. Be pleasant. Be humble. Be gentle.[THC 44]

    These are all goals or attributes of T'ai Chi as a practice. As you dance the energy spiral, you are relaxed, holding your body loosely and your attention softly unfocused looking past, beyond, within. Your tailbone is slightly tucked in, rotated under, by a slight bending of the knees. When you shift your weight forward or back, or from side to side, the shoulders are carried above the hips without leaning. All movements are gentle, slow and economical. It should take only 30-40 minutes to complete.

    It's not necessary to seek a place of beauty and serenity for the practice of the Dance of the Energy Spiral. You will develop your own serenity and beauty within that will allow you to tolerate, or even transform almost any external condition, even when you are not practicing. That happened to me one fine spring day on which the homeless in Minneapolis were protesting the refusal of HUD to release the excess inventory of HUD homes to civic groups who were seeking to find solutions to the growing homeless problem. My task was to provide food and landscaping materials and tools for those who were taking matters into their own hands by occupying abandoned residences.

    I had already delivered tools and food to my first stop and as I approached my second delivery destination, I could see police had already arrived at the Park Avenue house and were talking to the homeless leader at that residence. I calmly unloaded the boxes of food for distribution to the neighborhood, got out the flats of flowers that were going to be used to add some color and beauty to the property. I was planting petunias along the front sidewalk at the feet of the police and the accusations and warnings diminished to reasoned discussion and then the officers got a call from city hall to back off. The homeless set about improving the property, mowing the grass with the mowers I had brought, and distributing the food to neighbors, to introduce themselves in a neighborly way. Positive energy is a powerful and effective tool for bringing good things to life.

One of my favorite songs is The Wind, by Cat Stevens:
"I listen to the wind, to the wind of my soul.
Where I'll end up, well, I think only God really knows."

I discovered a variation in this movement meditation that I now call T'ai Chi for the Heart, which heals the heart and quiets the mind as well. One night on a teaching journey through Oklahoma, Texas, Arizona, and California, camped at Pismo Beach, I couldn't sleep because of a broken heart, so I walked onto a high sand dune overlooking the incoming tide on a moonlit Pacific shore. While doing T'ai Chi Chih, I 'accidentally' brought the energy to my heart chakra. My grieving heart was instantly relieved, almost as though it had been shocked. Now, as I complete a movement, I pause at my heart, and then continue to the next chakra below the navel, the T'an T'ien. A minor shift, but one that yields an amazing self-healing. I was able to feel the chi even stronger. Soon, my fingers would flutter like ribbons in a gentle breeze, without me trying to move them.

The Heart is the body's Fourth Chakra in Chinese medicine and serves as one of the most important centers for the distribution and storage of the subtle heart energy, quantum energy, whereas western medicine sees the brain as the core of the body's systems. With this brief change of form, after a few lessons and practice, you can feel an increased surge of energy into your heart chakra, helpful to those who have experienced heartbreak, emotional abuse, or low self-esteem. To feel love for others you need to first love yourself. That's unconditional love—agape.

Back in Minnesota, as a manager of Ed and Ruth Ann's organic farm, while doing T'ai Chi Chih on my deck I caught a glimpse at the corner of my eye of two hummingbirds darting at each other. Soon the victor of the bird fight was hovering inches from my navel. Looking down at him, I softly said "Hi, little one!" He looked up at me, as though he was expecting an immense flower to provide enormous quantities of nectar.

Immediately after he flew away, the second hummingbird was hovering in his place, as though expecting nectar. He looked up at me (as had the other) as though wondering where all the nectar was. I greeted him with a bright "Hi, little guy!" Then he, too, flew away.

Chi energy is REAL! The hummingbirds had apparently seen what my eyes were not able to see. That was a lesson not taught at university, but only taught in the laboratory of life, shown to me by the Grandmothers and Grandfathers who guide our footsteps and remind us to listen to the spirit wind, the sissagwad.

When I was living in south Minneapolis for a short time one of my housemates complained of a muscle spasm in his neck that had kept him awake the previous night. He was worried that if he didn't relieve the pain, he would not be able to sleep this night which would likely put him in an emergency crisis at a hospital the next day because of his diabetes. So, I showed him how to do three of the T'ai Chi Chih forms and told him to practice them before he went to bed. Next morning, he came down the stairs smiling.

"See Allen," as he easily rotated his head from side to side, "it worked! Thank you."

As you do the Dance of the Energy Spiral just be relaxed, holding your body loosely and your attention softly focused looking past, through, beyond, within. Your tailbone is slightly tucked in, rotated under by a slight bending of your knees. When you shift your weight forward or back, or from side to side, your shoulders should be carried above hands up to the side, keeping your elbows by your side moving your hips without leaning.

All movements are gentle, slow-motion, and economical, taking about 30-40 minutes to complete. You will not need to find a place of beauty or serenity for this practice. It comes with its own serenity and beauty within. Who you are will not become attached to the what around you.

Connecting Mother Earth And Father Sky

Your hands reach down to full extension lift energy from Mother Earth while breathing in and send it up to Father Sky (breathing out), sweeping arms down to sunset/sunrise horizons to your left and right (while breathing in), then bring your hands back to your heart while breathing in, bring the energy back to your heart while breathing in, then down to your birth connection while slowly breathing out. Continue immediately to the next action.

Sweeping The Energy Breeze

Turn your palms forward, sweep your arms forward and lifting up while breathing in, turn your palms down and breathe out while slowly lowering your arms to your side, hands slightly past your hips, and turn your hands forward.

Repeat 8 more times. Bring your hands from reaching forward back to your heart while breathing out, pause and feel the love as you breathe it in, then carry the energy down to your birth connection as you breathe out. Pause.

Eagle Flying

Bring your fingers and thumbs together at your birth connection, then bending your knees slightly, sweep your hands to the side keeping your elbows in at your side as you slowly breathe in. Sweep your hands back toward your birth connection while slowly breathing out. Repeat 1X. On the 2nd flap, rotate your hands at the wrist toward your body and then away. Do this set 4X. On the 4th set, after your hands return to your birth connection, breathe in as you raise your hands your hands up to your heart. Feel the love energy infusing your heart, then return your hands to your birth connection as you breathe out. Pause.

Soaring Over Mother Earth

With both hands palms down near your left shoulder and thumbs nearly touching, step forward on your left heel, trace a circle (breathing in) away from you and back to your heart (breathe out). Repeat slowly, breathing slowly each cycle in and out. On the 9th cycle, pause at your heart, feel the love energy, then carry the energy down to your birth connection. Pause. Repeat, starting from your right shoulder, shifting your weight to your right heel and moving your body forward, keep your shoulders and hips aligned. As you reach, your lead foot will be nearly flat on the floor while your back heel is rocked up slightly, massaging the bottom of your feet as you circle your hands.

***

Throwing The Ball

At your left shoulder, form a ball of energy with your hands, your fingertips, and thumbs not quite touching. Left heel forward, rock forward (as you breathe in), gently push the ball away by moving you're hands forward and release the energy by turning your palms downward, as you rock back (and you breathe out) bringing your hands to your heart. Repeat 9X. Pause. Repeat, starting from your right shoulder with your right heel forward, just a comfortable step out, not stretching far or stressing. shifting your weight onto your right heel and moving your body forward keeping your shoulders and hips aligned and as you reach comfortably reach your lead foot will be nearly flat to the floor while your back heel is now rocked up slightly. Lower your hands to your birth connection at the end of each set.

Around The Drum

Hands at your chest, palms and fingers not quite touching hold a ball of energy. Left heel forward. As your body moves forward slide your wrists down lightly brushing your body an then away when at your hip, then (breathing in) forward from your hips, up, and back. tracing an imaginary bass drum in front of you, back toward your chest and to your heart (breathing out). Feel the love energy entering your heart. Continue moving, slowly. Repeat 9X. On completing the 9th cycle, move the energy down to your birth connection (breathing out). Pause. Repeat for the right side from the right shoulder, shoulder and start with your right heel forward, just a comfortable step out, not stretching far or stressing, keeping your shoulders and hips aligned and as you reach comfortably, your lead foot will be nearly flat to the floor while your back heel is now rocked up slightly. On completing the 9th cycle, move the energy down to your birth connection (breathing out). Pause.

Daughter On The Mountain

Palms forward at each hip, left heel forward, bring your in a sweeping circle up past your face, left hand closest (breathing in) and continue to return to your waist (breathing out) as you rock back to place your weight on your right leg. On the 9th cycle bring your hands to your heart and feel the love energy (breathing in), then carry the energy down to your birth connection (breathing out). Pause. Repeat for the right side from the right shoulder, shoulder and start with your right heel forward, just a comfortable step out, not stretching far or stressing, keeping your shoulders and hips aligned. This time the closest hand to your face is the right and the hand farthest from your face in the simultaneous crossing is the left hand. On completing the 9th cycle, (breathing in) move the energy down to your birth connection (breathing out). Pause.

Daughter In The Valley

Palms forward at each shoulder, left heel forward, reach while breathing in to caress the love energy between your hands without touching as you settle back onto your right heel (breathing out). Bring your hands full of love energy back to your heart and reposition your hands at the shoulders to get more of that love energy, 9X. After the 9th cycle, (breathing in) move the energy down to your birth connection (breathing out). Pause. Repeat for the right side by palms forward at each shoulder, right heel forward, reach forward (breathing in). Move the energy down to your birth connection (breathing out). Pause.

* * *

Carry The Energy Ball

At your right shoulder cup your hands around an 'energy' ball, fingers up. Stepping left with your left heel, carry the ball down (breathing in) and up around and past your face (breathing out) while shifting your weight with each side-step 3X. On the third side-step, bring your right foot to the left. Immediately drop your hands to your birth connection and circle up to your right shoulder. Repeat side stepping and carrying the ball of energy. When the energy ball reaches your heart on the 3rd step, carry the energy ball down to your birth connection and cup your hands around a second energy ball at your left shoulder. Stepping right with your right heel, repeat these movements to the right. On the 3rd step, hold the energy ball to your heart and absorb the energy. Then carry the energy to your birth connection. Pause.

Push-Pull

Holding your palms forward at each shoulder, step out on your left heel. Moving forward, push your hands away, slightly down and away, as you breathe in. As you rock back (spine held vertically), turn your hands palms toward you, and bring energy to your heart, (breathing out) 9X. Repeat, holding your palms forward at each shoulder, step out on with your right heel.

Receiving The Energy Of Father Sky

Hands cupped and open at your left shoulder with palms up with little fingers almost touching, left heel forward, trace a circle forward and around (breathing in) back to your heart (breathing out) palms and fingers toward your heart. Continue smoothly, slowly breathing in as you step forward with your left heel and breathing out as you return to your heart. On the 9th time, pause at your heart, feel the love energy. Then carry the energy down to your birth connection. Pause. Repeat, starting from your right shoulder leading on your right heel. 9X and pause.

Caressing The Energy

Holding a ball of energy at your birth connection. right hand above your left almost touching, step left with your left heel. (breathing in) Moving slowly your right hand remains in place as your left hand moves left with your body. As you bring your right leg left to bring it together with your left, bring both hands to your heart, (breathing out). Then palms down, (breathing in) carry the energy down to your birth connection (breathing out) 4X. Immediately, turn your hands so your left is over the right but not touching, step right on your right, your left hand remaining in place as your right hand moves right with your body (breathing in). As your left leg steps right to bring your legs together, bring both hands to your heart (breathing out). 4X. Then palms down, (breathing in) carry the energy to your birth connection (breathing out). Pause.

T'ai Chi While Lying Down

These exercises are all done with coordinated deep breathing in which inhalation is exaggerated by expanding belly as much as possible, hold for a count of three (about 3 seconds) and exhalation by flattening belly as much as possible, and hold for a count of three, (about 3 seconds.) This will bring a lot of healing oxygen to your body.

These exercises are not intended to push outside your comfort zone. There's no need to do these exercises rapidly.

Just lying on your back you can accomplish much of what you can by standing. Be gentle and loving toward yourself and enjoy the gentle movement. It's like a graceful dance with yourself and your inner being.

Practice 4 or 5 breaths to begin. While breathing in, flex your feet by pointing your toes toward the foot of the bed gently without exertion. While breathing out flex your toes and foot back toward your head and smile at them, then breath out. Gently repeat flexing 4 or 5 times and smile at this little game you are playing with your toes. If you like, you might thank them for playing this game with you, silently, if you prefer. They can hear you without sounds.

As you breath in, gently lift one leg. Just a little bit. As you breath out, lower your leg back down to rest on the bed. Only lift as much as is comfortable. Repeat these 4 or 5 times and then repeat this with the other leg. Do your legs deserve another smile? At least give yourself a smile. You deserve it. It's the breathing in synch with the movement that is what this is intended to accomplish.

Gently bend both knees and place the bottom of your feet on the bed. As you breath in, point your toes so your heels are raised from the bed. Hold for 3 seconds, then breath out as you let your heels come to rest on the bed while your toes curl back and point up. Hold for 3 seconds, while breathing out.

Gently bend both knees and place the bottom of your feet on the bed. As you breath in, slowly, gently lift one leg as far as is comfortable, counting to 3 for 3 seconds, then breath out as you let your foot slowly return to the bed. Then repeat this with the other leg. Do these 4 or 5 times slowly, switching the leg that is lifted while continuing the synchronized breathing.

To bring strength and mobility to the hip, start with both legs bent at the knee, feet a little bit apart. Then slowly inhaling, gently collapse both knees together to the right, on a count of 3, then slowly back up on a count of 3 as you slowly exhale, again at a count of 3. Finally, slowly inhaling on a count of 3, slowly collapse your knees to the left. This should gently twist your hip slightly. Then slowly bring both knees back up as you breathe in. Do this 4 or 5 times slowly. A smile would let your knees know how well they did.

With feet apart about the width of your shoulders, begin to inhale as you gently lift your hips on a count of 3 as much as you can comfortably, perhaps just a little bit, hold for a count of 3, then exhale as you slowly let you hips down to the bed on a count of 3, and pause for a count of 3. Repeat 4 or 5 times.

With knees bent so feet are flat to the bed, and arms near your side, slightly bent and curved slightly over tummy. As you slowly breathe in, your arms slowly swing a little bit away from your body until at a count of 3 your abdomen has risen, and your ribs have lifted. Hold for a count of 3, then begin a slow exhale on a count of 3, letting your hands slowly follow the emptying of your lungs and your tummy relaxes fully and hold for 3 seconds. Repeat 4 or 5 times.

Remaining on your back, knees up or down, imagine a ball of energy that your hands will carry back and forth across your chest. Slowly carrying the ball of energy from left to right on a count of 3, your right hand is near your chin facing away from your face. Your left hand is closer to your tummy turned up toward your chin. Reaching the right, pause for 3 seconds. Switching from carrying the ball of energy left to the right, you will have to switch your hands from carrying the ball of energy to the right, your left hand is closer to your chin and your right is closer to your tummy. As you carry the ball left to right, slowly inhale and when the ball has reached the right, pause for 3 seconds, switch hands so that once again the left is near the chin and your right is nearer the tummy, carry the ball of energy from right to left as you slowly exhale. Going right you're inhaling and left you're exhaling.

On your back, knees up or down, slowly lift energy from your tummy with cupped hands moving up toward your head, as you inhale on a count of 3. When you reach your head, pause on a count of 3, turn your hands to push and spread the energy over your chest and tummy, on a count of 3 as your cupped hands slowly move toward your navel. Reaching your navel, pause 3 seconds and turn your hands back toward your head once again. Repeat 6 or 7 times.

You can view this whole procedure on YouTube: https://www.youtube.com/watch?v=fpA4aWjI_HU

The Spirals whirled even faster.
"He has listened and has danced a new dream for his people," smiled a Grandmother.
"His heart is true!" celebrated a Grandfather. "He accomplished what he promised!"
"We nearly lost him when he had that stroke in Australia!" cried the Dreamkeeper. "And that heart attack in Vancouver when he was in the right place at the right time with the right people."
"He always had Us, his spirit helpers, to keep him on track and get him in a place where he could reflect and write his books!" sang a little one. "Even then he almost missed the big revelation of the train on the tracks." rumbled the Gatekeeper.

Surviving The Micronova

Ben Davidson writes, "The Earth is due for another catastrophe cycle, and the evidence of its unfolding can be seen throughout the solar system and beyond, and most intimately here on Earth."[OS 58]

Eventually the changes we are seeing will result in a solar micronova, rapid geomagnetic reversal, crustal shifts and/or Earth tilt, continental tsunamis, major earthquakes, and the disappearance of several species amidst a 10-50% overall hit to the biosphere. Human civilization is expected to be especially hard-hit due to its reliance on electricity (which will not be available for 10s to 100s of years after the event) and overwhelming proximity to coastlines."[OS 58]

Your chances for survival are primarily influenced by the population of your area, its latitude, how close you are to a coastline, and your attitude and capacity to focus on survival. While waiting for the Earth and sun to begin showing the onset of the event, the weakening of the magnetosphere might affect agriculture, technology, climate, earthquakes, and volcanoes. War, rioting, climate, drought, flooding, more active seismic zones, are all the more likely. If you're in a flood plain or near one, lava from a local volcano might fill that before it reaches where you live, or the tsunami might flood that before the water gets to you. You might also need protection from winds and tornadoes as the weather gets wild.

When the poles shift, much more of Russia will be closer to the new equator that will span the Arctic Ocean. Europe will be largely desert when the Equator runs through western Europe, Scandinavia, Italy, across the Mediterranean and between Libya and Algeria. Antarctica is also likely to be at the new equator.[NEW 35]

Where do you plan to be when the poles flip? The Gulf of Mexico will slosh north, the Atlantic will slosh over much of Europe and the eastern USA. The Pacific will hit the north coasts of Australia and Indonesia. Then the sloshback tsunamis go the opposite way, hitting eastern Canada, northern South America, West Africa southern Australia, India, and China from the south.

The age of electricity will be over for many years. Imagine camping for the rest of your life? No fuel for your chainsaw, pump for your well… got a river nearby? Gotta know where all that is and how you will handle it.

Got pails? Know how to efficiently start a fire? Got the tinder? Kindle a fire without matches or lighters? Did you include a way to cut wood? Dig a protective shelter? A well? Sew on a button?

Low Population/Low Crime—If you live in a large city, you've had a peek at what chaos will look like from the riots televised during the "summer of love," as the Mayor of Seattle called it. Now just imagine if there was no electricity… or water… or food. It wasn't limited to large cities—you remember Kenosha, WI? Fear breeds anger and desperation. Not a safe place to be. No wall/open border cartels with Mexico, even NEAR big cities. Big Cities will be death traps, even trying to get out of one when others have the same idea. What would you call a place with hungry scared people? Emotional instability is more common under geomagnetic storm and extreme cosmic ray conditions, as if we needed any other stressors in the environmental index. Add to that, a geomagnetic excursion that happens every 12,000 years. If you know of Satanism in an area, such as the Denver Airport, you might wisely avoid such areas. Foothills of the Rockies might be safer from the criminality as well as the Inertial Tsunami.

Seismic Area/Volcanoes and/or Fault Lines—There are about 1,350 potentially active volcanoes worldwide, of which about 500 have erupted in historical time. Most of them are in the Ring Of Fire around the Pacific Ocean. There are 161 potentially active volcanoes in the United States and its territories. The United States ranks third, behind Indonesia and Japan. Indonesia will be near the new North Pole and uninhabitable. The Caspian range north from Greece is volatile, but east of the Caspian Sea would likely have survivors. Japan has elevation mostly from volcanic mountains and will be hit by great Pacific Inertial Tsunamis and unsurvivable.

Inertial Tsunami—Because the water of oceans, seas, and large lakes or inland seas are likely to slosh out of their coastlines when the rotation of the Earth slows and stops briefly, it might be better to not try to outguess the direction or elevation the inertial tsunami will rise. It would be much less risky to assemble a raft made of plastic drums as a flotation craft. However, you won't have much control with winds around 100 mph, turbulent water, and wild currents. A life vest might be a great precaution. This might be more vital near a coast than mid-continent. A few 10x10 plastic tarps might be useful as sail, water-collecting devices, or a temporary roof to keep you dry in the rain or snow. Try to always be ready to game it out in your mind. There is also the possibility of unpredictable tectonic events with the unlocking of the low velocity zone, followed by crustal plates moving or sinking, and sliding under other plates. All kinds of geological mayhem could create many surprises, so total awareness with thorough preparation could make all the difference between survival and misfortune.

If the thermoelectric linkage between the crust and mantle lets go, whole continents can delink and move about, changing the way your landmarks were once located. The plumes and other formations of the LLSVP are the hidden and unknown factor buried out of sight in the mantle, unpredictable like lightning and impactors from the micronova. All you can do is the best you can to prepare, learn, stay clearly focused. "Eyes open, no fear" is a survivor's attitude that Ben Davidson would always remind us, after another of his daily space weather newsclips.

If you are in the Americas or South Africa, this Inertial Tsunami is likely to come from the south. In Australia and Siberia, it will come from the north. However, how will you know North… or South? As I write this, my compass shows a deflection of nearly 40 deg. It's ok for now, but when the poles continue to move and the Sun novas, all bets are off. A compass will only be useful if you have some stars or constellations to guide you. The poles will move, remember. Get to know some of the geography of the heavens. Sunrise might not be in what you once called 'east'.

The Alps and Pyrenee Mountain ranges might provide sufficient elevation to survive the tsunami in Europe just as the Adirondacks, Alleghenies, and Great Smokies of the Appalachian Range can protect East Coast Americans.

'Head for the hills!' will have new meaning. Mountains of the West Coast are likely to be erupting and the San Andreas and New Madrid faults will not be the only faults to create surprises—it's an endangered area to avoid. Disneyland will be gone, and Disney World in Florida will be under the deluge.

Slosh-back Tsunami—After the inertial tsunami has subsided there can be a return, or sloshback tsunami as ocean levels equalize. Major sloshback will hit the Atlantic provinces of Eastern Canada, the Gulf Coast of South America, the Atlantic coast of West Africa, the southern coast of Australia, India, and China. Queensland might prepare for the inertial tsunami from the north, whereas coastal Western Australia, South Australia, Victoria, and New South Wales should be wary of a sloshback tsunami from the south. Similarly, Hudson Bay in Canada can experience a sloshback on the south coast of the bay. The Pacific will slosh back from Alaska to hit the West coast from the north. The eastern coast of Brazil is vulnerable to Atlantic sloshback. The southern tip of Argentina is vulnerable to both Atlantic and Pacific Inertial Tsunamis.

Too Cold In The Future—The Bay of Bengal will probably be the North Pole through the next cycle, so India will be more suitable for seals and polar bears than cows, and Southeast Asia more friendly to reindeer and penguins than elephants and monkeys. The Taj Mahal and Angkor Wat will be buried in glacial ice. Ecuador will need a new name and the Amazon will lose its jungle. Brazil might get as chilly as northern Canada. The Panama Canal will likely be icebound most of the year. The Rocky Mountains will protect from tsunamis, but they will be quite cold. Survivors will likely be found south of Mexico City, on Madagascar, in eastern, southwest, and central Australia, the Argentine

Andes, the Horn of Africa, mountains of northern India and Mongolia (but too cold to stay there). The safest place in UK is the Welsh Highlands. London is in a drainage zone—the River Thames. It could be 100-300 feet deeper for a few days and moving at about 100 mph [the torrent of London!]. Higher altitudes will mean colder temperatures. The shock of this event can halt normal functioning in most people—it doesn't have to be you. You at least have been given more time to prepare than most.

"For the first time, faith and prophecy can be observed by observable reality and scientific proof. We have arrived at a place where science demands the ancient stories be true. Science fiction writers would be hard-pressed to conceive of the harmony painted by the Sun, the Earth, and the scientific journals, and it is not fiction. We are all the main characters in the most incredible version of the greatest story ever told, and we are approaching the big scene of the production."—Ben Davidson[OS 58]

I began a search for mines in my county and found several only a few miles away. Some were over 5,000' up the mountain. Next, I'll be looking for caves, tunnels, and fallout shelters, anything underground. I've seen maps that show extensive and deep networks of tunnels. Some who have studied this problem estimate that in the USA there are enough deep tunnels for 10-500 million people. In other parts of the world, there are entire underground cities probably dug by people who needed to find safety during past micronovas.

Our urban lifestyle has eroded our inherited capacity to survive. Those who maintained a connection to the outdoors through camping, hunting, fishing, and hiking, may have an advantage of experience and knowledge, but most important is the instinctual wisdom. Changing our focus to survival while we have time, we can hone those skills with more time spent in real life experiences in nature, practicing those survival skills, honing them to a fine edge that can make a huge difference when the time arrives that we need to have those skills on the fine edge of ready. The malfunction of one small part of our technology can bring down the protective edifice we call civilization. We need a sense of what we must do for ourselves that can keep us safe, ready, healthy, aware, and alive. In the meantime, we will bolster our sense of self-preservation, critical to our self-confidence.

Survival education is a way to enhance harmony with the wilderness—the wildness that lives at our doorstep. There is an exhilaration and inner peace with the familiarity and interaction with the natural world. We will be needing that awe and respect for the forces of nature before they are forced upon us. Wilderness is a vast, powerful resource in our crash course in survival. Learn and grow in self-reliance, no longer at the effect of whatever catastrophe that might come along.

First, you must decide to live! Once you've made that decision, survival is natural just doing what you gotta. It's elementary, but essential. A will to live is simply related to your sense that you have more you want to experience in this world of time and space. Heaven can wait!

Practical Survival

In your emergency survival kit, include a few granola snack bars to eat until you can find food by traps, foraging for edible vegetation, or fishing. Line, hooks, and small bobbers are good additions to your survival kit. You should also have drinking water in your emergency survival kit to get to your next goal (shelter), and a fire started to allow you to sleep through the night, and you brought a roll of clear plastic to block moisture from the ground, which can also be used to get clean drinking water when spread over a pit dug to expose damp soil. That's for tomorrow, there's no sun at night to make it work.

You need to get into shelter ASAP to recover from the stress of the cataclysm. An abandoned vehicle might be tempting, but metal is a poor insulator. Creating a snow cave for shelter might not be wise if a solar flare might flash it into a puddle. Better to create a minimal Earth shelter next to a fallen tree or boulder with your folding shovel or hand trowel. Burrow into the loose soil, leaves, or evergreen needles or find a hollow log. Leaning brush, chunks of bark, or evergreen branches against a fallen tree or boulder will also create a temporary shelter for a night. Your poncho can also make a simple shelter.

Fire

A fire not only prevents death by hypothermia, but it also provides security and comfort that allows the mind to return to rational and practical solutions that can assure safety and survival. Firefighters have occasionally used this survival technique. After the fire has burned down to embers, sweep away the embers and ash with a sapling. Replace with several inches of dry loose soil and you can sleep in comfort on the nice warm ground. Of course, you brought sleeping bag or blankets, didn't you?

If you can first warm up the ground with a toasty fire and scrape away the embers and ash with a tree branch, the residual warmth in the soil could keep you comfy for the night. You did remember to include a zip lock bag of firestarter, and either a small lighter, matches in a waterproof container, or a spark-striker in your survival kit, didn't you?

You will have practiced starting fires many times before. You know that small twigs are stacked like a little teepee with a little nook to receive a pinch of fine tinder that is easy to start on fire, which can easily start the twigs on fire, then larger branches, then logs. Enjoy the protection fire affords from predators looking for food, you. Natural tinder can include milk weed pods, dry heads of cattails, pitch oozing from a pine tree, or even wood-shavings scraped from a pitchy piece of wood. Nests of small birds or mammals can provide both tinder and small twigs to start a fire. The best site for a fire is protected from wind and rain, preferably in a place that has materials for building shelter.

Firefighters also know that in a wildfire, the fire tends to burn up hills, so don't try to outrun a wildfire that is going uphill, it will win. If trapped by a fire, try to find a damp area, a pond or swamp, or even a spot bare of flammable materials. Get close to the ground, face down in the dirt. Breathing the hot air of the fire can sear the delicate tissues in your lungs. If you can, breathe through a wet shirt. If you're in water, dunk your head to keep your hair from catching on fire, try to cover as much as you can. Much of the world might be burning on the sun side of Earth. Be wary. Eyes open, no fear, keep your cool, be safe.

Check your environment for any branches above you that could loosen at night and fall on you. Always remain vigilant and wary of dangers when you are awake. A small, dry cave can be a first-class shelter if you find one. You might need a windbreak wall to prevent wind chill. Flat rocks, brush, even armloads of grass can block the wind. If it has a sunny exposure, it will be warmer than if no sun shines in at all.

Shelter

A wattle-work shelter is a double frame of woven branches between which you can insert moss or leaves for insulation that also creates a barrier against the wind. Such a wall can be used to provide a comfortable hut. You can construct it in a circle and add a domed roof of bent saplings for the strongest of shelters, adding slabs of bark for protection from the rain and snow.

Round shelters are easier to build, more economical, require less material, and are stronger. They withstand wind better. Two wattle-walls connected as an L can provide a windbreak at your front door in which an open fire for heat or cooking can be safely used. Adding a third wall can enclose space, and a lean-to that can be roofed with more branches. And that tarp you brought along can provide protection from rain or snow, covered with a few layers of evergreen boughs or slabs of bark to add insulation, and protect the tarp from wind.

Standing in the center of the space you have chosen, use a long stick to mark a circle, perhaps starting with a 10-12' diameter, (about 4 big steps across). Cut sturdy 10' long saplings with an angle cut at the bottom. Ask each sapling for its permission before you cut it down. Listen with your heart. Place two sets of saplings on the east and west sides. Be sure to notice where the sun sets and rises. These will be your morning door and your end-of-the-day door, to allow the sun to shine in to greet the day and warm you.

Bury the butt end of each sapling 8-10" deep. Using a sturdy, pointed 2–3 foot stake, pound it into the ground about 12", work it around to loosen the soil, pull it out and push a sapling in and tamp the soil with a blunt stick. To make the saplings bow outward, angle the butt ends slightly inward. When they are brought together, they will be almost vertical. Bend the doorway saplings toward each other so that the two ends overlap at least 1 foot and lash them together with cordage you brought with you. When the east-west saplings are tied securely, add the north and south until all saplings are tied at the peak. Now weave the less sturdy saplings horizontally starting at the base and working toward the peak, each ring about 1 foot apart on the vertical sides and about 9" apart at the roof to the peak.

This will allow you to use sheaves of reeds, cattails, or slabs of bark over the top to shed the rain and keep you dry. A tarp, if you have one, can add extra protection from the rain. As you have time, you can stuff dried grass into the wattle wall and even into the roof before you cover it. Keep the door openings small, perhaps 4-5 feet high so that easy access with an arm load is comfortable.

An L-shaped wattle-wall alcove at each entrance will reduce cold inside. You might want to provide an opening at the peak to allow for adequate ventilation. A ten-foot diameter shelter can sleep up to 4 people. Bunk beds can be made with vertical supports that go to the ceiling. These also make useable shelves.

Once the outside is completed, wattled walls inside can add warmth and comfort, doors can be fashioned to enclose the space from the cold or predators, roofing mats can be sewn together. Hides and blankets hung on the walls add more insulation. Sleeping benches can be constructed around the perimeter to provide ample seating, workspace, and storage underneath. These are supported with chair-height frames of forked sticks and horizontal wall beam supports of the wall. After the shelter is built, dig a shallow trench around it to drain run-off from the roof away from the shelter.

A Bed

A comfortable bed can be made of cattail stalks, sagebrush branches, or dry grass laid over a bed of woven saplings. I fondly remember a night I slept under the stars on a bed of drying sagebrush—aromatic as well as comfortable. Even in winter, dry grass can be found in protected niches, at the base of trees, windswept slopes, often blown into caves or crannies. Doing a smudge ceremony is good medicine as well as prayers to the trees that are providing you shelter.

Again, you can build a fire on the ground and heat it for the comfy warm night's sleep you will need. Don't build too thoroughly air-tight—you don't want to create a carbon monoxide problem. A fire of any kind in an air-tight shelter presents a deadly problem. Don't let candles or Sterno burn all night. You need to pay attention to little details like that. "Eyes open. No Fear. Be safe everyone," Ben Davidson would intone.

Water

Water is vital! The last time we survived a micronova, water in the wilderness was not polluted. This time we don't have the luxury, or the capacity to safely drink from streams or ponds. Polluted water is now common even in remote wilderness. Even spring water could be contaminated and must be purified, but we can get purified water to drink through a distillation process that uses no electricity or batteries, if you brought that clear plastic, that would do all the work with help from the sun. That clear plastic you slept on can also be used to extract pure water from damp soil, preferably a dark loam, rather than rocky or sandy soils that don't hold much moisture, although damp plant material can also provide condensing moisture.

Dig a pit about 18" deep by about 3 feet wide in a sunlit area. Place a container in the bottom. Create a cone shape solar still by placing the clear plastic sheet over the pit, carefully anchoring the edges with the soil from the pit and placing a small rock above the container to shape the plastic sheet into a cone shape. As the sun shines through the clear plastic, water will evaporate from the soil in the pit and collect on the underside of the plastic, gather in little droplets that run down the plastic drawn to a point by the small rock, and collect in a small cup at the bottom. Most of the work is done by the sun so, you can just watch your drinking water collect. It might even get so hot that the rock must be wrapped in bark to keep it from melting through the plastic sheet.

Such a still could yield 1-2 quarts of water/day. You need about a gallon daily, so you can set up a second still. In rain, even more water would collect on the upper side of the plastic sheet. If you thought to bring a straw, you could drink that water without disturbing the collection on the underside of the still. The still will continue to work through the night at half the collection rate. Water is a primary resource humans must master to survive.

Food For Survival

Food is the least important requirement for survival. A healthy person can live three weeks or more without food if inactive. But work, travel, or cold put greater demands on the body. Finding edible foods in the wild can be a daunting task, but in the days of Euell Gibbons, I would take my science students on a neighborhood hike to find edible foods, even wild asparagus. The asparagus, I brought back to eat for my lunch. We found cattails, leaves of linden, dandelion, and others I no longer remember. Each hike was about 40 minutes long and we would always find many edible plants.

I even showed them how to tap maple trees to gather the sap that I tried to concentrate by the traditional boiling method, but in my school lab the process was taking too long and leaving the hotplate on warm overnight yielded a school filled with acrid smoke and a fire engine outside when I got to school the next morning. The sap had reached a critical point overnight when I could not remain and before I was able to return, it was too late. Oops! You will have the option to watch over the boiling down process through the night to avoid that problem.

Edible Plants

There are many thousands of edible plants, and they vary widely from one ecosystem to another. Excellent guides are available, and their study and use is highly recommended before settling on a preferred location to survive the micronova in an unfamiliar location. Now is the time to try to learn the local, edible plants. There will be a test and the passing grade is survival. Food grows wherever humans have settled. Here are some edible herbs that can be found across the United States and preferred by our great-grandmothers and great-grand-fathers.

Acorns helped several Native American cultures survive in eastern USA. The very best acorns are from oak trees that have rounded leaves, the white oak family. The first step after collection is to put the acorns in water and discard the ones that float. To crack these nuts, use pliers with one of its jaws on the nearly flat top, the other jaw on the pointed tip. Crack them the long way, then squeeze the nut at its tips and pop the meat out whole. Tannin is the chemical that makes the acorn taste bitter. After 2 hours of boiling and a change of water whenever the boiling water turns yellowish, the acorn meats can be dried and pounded into fine meal.

Dry the acorns gradually inside your home at ambient temperatures. The acorns should be spread out on trays one layer thick. This drying method takes 2-4 weeks. Or place the tray of acorns in direct sunlight for 2-5 days, longer if the temps are cold or if the days are not completely sunny. Dry until the acorns turn brown, or they will very soon be covered in mold. Otherwise pound the meats into fine meal and then place meal in a porous, cloth bag, and pour boiling water through it. Use like cornmeal or mix with any flour or make acorn cakes mixing 2 cups cornmeal with ¼ cup water, and ½ tsp salt, let stand about 1 hour, then heat 3 Tbsp cooking oil in frying pan. Drop batter into oil to make cakes 3" across, set pan at reduced heat and brown slowly on both sides, eat hot or cold. Keeps for several days.

If the acorns are not to be used immediately check them again in a week and discard any acorns that are molding. Mold will spread rapidly. Trying to save an extra acorn can cause you to lose the entire collection. Check again in a week. Store in small airtight containers or Ziplock bags.

Freezing is a better way to store them if the weather has suddenly turned cold. Shell out the meat of the acorn and freeze in Ziplock bags. Acorn meat will last much longer this way. The dried acorns still in their original shell will remain edible for many months and can help you feed yourself into the winter months.

From SW Maine and extreme southern Quebec, west to southern Ontario, central Michigan, to southeastern Minnesota; south to western Iowa, eastern Kansas, Oklahoma, and Texas; east to northern Florida and Georgia. The other common oak has pinnate leaves that are pointed instead of round. Red oaks have more tannin, which require more changes of water. Eastern USA to Colorado, Nebraska, and Oklahoma, and the Pacific NW.

Amber Jelly Roll Mushroom (Exidia Recisa) is bland but edible. Being available during the winter months makes them particularly valuable as a food source. Look on hardwood debris for a blob of brownish jelly on sticks, stumps, and logs. Cooked in a soup or stew you will hardly notice them. Cut up into little pieces they help add substance to the meal. Fairly common and widely distributed across the northern hemisphere, including throughout Britain and Ireland as well as most of mainland Europe, northern Asia USA and Canada.

***

Arrowhead (Sagittaria Latifolia) has a large leaf shaped like an arrowhead growing in marshes, in wet soil along creeks and in ditches. In spring the tubers, seedpods, leaves and stalks can be edible. Dig them with your toes, the tubers float to the surface when they are dislodged. Edible raw, they are better boiled or baked, replacing potatoes If they are peeled before eating. Seedpods provide a food source in the fall. All of USA except Nevada, All of Canada south of 60 degrees. Look at the leaf veins. If there are only three, it is toxic. If there are many, it's safe.

You can find **Asparagus** from 5-6' tall wispy stalks that might have tiny bright red berries that you can plant in your garden. In spring, shoots come up from the roots. Those can be broken off and taken home for a light boil—a delectable vegetable for your delight. Native to the eastern Mediterranean lands and Asia Minor. Commonly grows wild over much of that territory today, also in the trans-Caucasus, Europe, and even in many places in the United States where it has escaped from cultivation.

Blackberries are the king of all wild berries and their habit as a creeping, vining shrub conquers more territory every year, protected by thorns, producing best in half-day sun. Its prolific, tart berries, sometimes an inch long, ripen in July or August. use raw on cereal or in jellies, jams, syrups, or juices, add to cakes, muffins and pancakes or eat raw from the bush. Eastern North America and on the Pacific coast and cultivated in many areas of North America and Europe.

The hollow pithy stems of **Blue Elderberry** identify this 6-20' erect, woody shrub with opposing saw-tooth leaves, that blooms during summer in flat-topped white-creamy clusters becoming small bluish-black berries ripe in September, good for wine or eaten raw, baked in muffins, pie, or pancakes. The blossoms can be dipped in batter and pan-fried during summer. Called Tree of Music by tribes that ram the pith out of the center and drill holes like a clarinet using fingers to choose notes. North and South America, Europe, and Asia.

Bullrush (Typha Angustifolia) grows in the shallow water of a marsh from rhizome in the bottom muck. Young shoots are edible raw. Older parts can be peeled to the tender core which can be eaten raw in a salad or boiled and sautéed. The young roots can be eaten like slender sweet potato or boiled for several hours to make a sugary sweet syrup. Older roots can be cut, dried and ground to make flour. Remove fibers before storing. Its pollen and ground seeds can be added to other preparations. Stems make great thatch for your roof. USA and Alaska, Canada except Nunavut and Baffin Island.

Cattails (Typha Sativa) can be harvested all year, are plentiful and easy to find near water, in shallow water, not to be mistaken for the similar roots and stem of the toxic wild Iris. You can dig up roots even during the cold months, which taste like a fibrous sweet potato or squash. Roots can be skinned and added to soup for thickening. In early spring, young stalks and dormant sprouts around the roots are edible raw. Just pull up a plant and peel back the leaves to find the young, tender core, which can also be added to a salad. Stalks and tender blooms can be cooked in a little water until tender and eaten like corn-on-the-cob or scrape the green buds off and use them in a casserole.

When you find the pollen has ripened, collect the buds, sift through the pollen to remove foreign debris and you can use the pollen in baking or sprinkled in any dish for added nutrition. Fresh cattail reeds can be woven into floor mats or bundled and tied to make thick sleeping mats, or coiled or woven baskets, or thatch for roofs or insulate walls of the shelter. All of USA and central Alaska-southern Canada south of 60° in maritime provinces, Kamchatka, coastal Siberia, Southern Russia, Ukraine, Europe, UK, Turkey, Levant.

Chokecherry has a bit of a pucker to the taste, but they are excellent thirst-quenchers, just spit out the stone/seed. Often a large shrub, it can be a small tree up to 25' tall. Oval, pointed, dark-green leaves have fine-toothed margins. White blossoms in show up in May, after the leaves are nearly grown. In August, the red-purple berries bend the branches under the heavy loads. Makes a fine drink or jelly. Northern USA and Southern Canada.

Clover is a protein-rich food, difficult to digest raw, but can be pan-fried with a bit of butter, boiled, or the flowers steeped as a tea. White clover in the north is non-toxic, but possibly toxic in southern regions. Red-flowered clover is not a problem. Red clover is native to Europe, Western Asia, and northwest Africa, but it has been naturalized in other continents, such as North and South America.

Common Chickweed can be harvested all year, it's plentiful. No toxics that resemble it, the entire plant is edible. Add to salads or to soups in the last few minutes, so it doesn't overcook, or blanche and add 1:1 to pancake batter for a greens pancake. USA, except for Texas, Oklahoma, Kansas. Alabama, Florida, and Carolinas, all of Canada, and Greenland.

In early spring, young **Dandelion** leaves are very tender

and make a good salad. Later they can be boiled, perhaps with a change of water to get rid of the bitterness that develops later in the season. Later in the season the whole plant including flowers can be boiled for 10 minutes, change water, and boil another 10 minutes. Flowers can also be dipped in batter and fried. Now naturalized throughout North America, southern Africa, South America, New Zealand, Australia, and India. It occurs in all 50 states of the US and most Canadian provinces.

Gooseberry grows to about 4-6', is ripe in July and August with wine-black edible berries mixed with some that are green. Tart but delicious raw, in sauces, jams, or pies —but beware the spine at each joint. American gooseberries are native to northeastern and north-central United States and the adjacent regions of Canada. Gooseberries are native to the Caucasus Mountains and North Africa, but might have escaped from cultivation. The woods near my childhood home offered gooseberries that would take all day to pick.

High-bush Cranberry (Viburnum Edule) is an erect shrub with leaves shaped like a maple and turn red in fall. May-June it blooms with showy clusters or small white florets which become clusters of red berries in August. which in some areas hang on after the leaves fall. They are juicy and sweetly tart eaten raw.an excellent a flavorful jelly, wine, or syrup on pancakes. High Bush Cranberry is found throughout the northern United States and Canada, from Alaska to central Oregon in the west.

Lamb's Quarters (Chenopodium) species are all over the US growing 3-6' high. Green stems sometimes have a red streak, leaves can be up to 4" long, a pudgy triangle. A white powdery down coats the underside of the leaves. Their mild, spinach flavor makes them a favorite wild green that can be eaten raw for its vitamins A and C. Heating destroys the vitamin C. Throughout North America, where its range extends from Canada south to Michoacán, Mexico, found in every US continental state.

Wild Mint smells like mint—add a sparkle to a meal. As a tea it can be served hot or cold. Leaves can be collected and dried, set aside for later use. In colder climates its soft stems and leaves die back completely with the 1st hard frost and new growth appears next season when the weather warms. Wild mints are native to the Himalaya and eastern Siberia, and North America.

Mulberries are a tree fruit that ripen May-July. Red berries on the east coast, but white mulberries have gone wild country wide. But raw leaves and unripe fruit are mildly toxic, causing hallucinations and stomach upset—unpleasant, if not lethal. You cannot afford to be at less than peak performance so be wary of unripe fruit or leaves. Ontario, Minnesota, and Vermont south to southern Florida, and west as far as southeastern South Dakota, Nebraska, Kansas, and central Texas.

Plantain like to grow flat to the ground and shoot up spikes covered with tiny flowers. A delightful base for a salad, plantains beg for more flavoring when cooked. Young new leaves that appear throughout the growing season can be harvested for salad. Seeds can be gathered to dry and grind into flour that can be used in any baking recipe. USA western Alaska, southern Canada, and Greenland.

Prickly Lettuce has tiny spines along the leaves and

lower stem. Young leaves resemble dandelion, but if you find one without the little spines, it is wild lettuce. Both can be eaten, fresh or boiled. Wild lettuce is better as a pain medicine from the milky substance found in the stems and leaves. Lower 48 in USA, southern Canada, Mexico, Argentina, Australia, South Africa, and Europe.

Purslane is another low-growing, ground-hugging green loaded with nutrients you can boil for 10 minutes and have a quick worthwhile meal. Or you can pick the leaves later when edible vegetation is scarce. Lower 48 in USA, Canada, Europe, India, China, Australia, New Zealand, Siberia, and South Korea.

Serviceberry varies from a scrubby bush to large shrub to small tree up to 15'. Showy white blossoms in April and May mature as red to blue-black berries early in summer. Used for an ingredient in pemmican, they can be dried and pounded into loaves. Fresh berries can be added to pancakes, muffins, pies, prepared as jams or jellies. Eastern USA and Canada and coastal Washington and BC.

Strawberries in the wild tend to be sparse and best used as a snack while foraging or can be combined with other fruit. A fine taste treat when you can find them. Low-growing, 3-16" high. Most of USA and Canada.

Thimbleberries grow on thornless shrubs 4-7' in damp soil and along streams in western regions. In July and August, white flowers become edible bright red cap-like berries that are sweetly tart and soft. Add to cakes, muffins and pancakes, or raw from the bush. Massachusetts, Quebec, Upper Midwest, Rocky Mtns to Western Alaska.

Watercress grows in abundance in slow-moving clear

creeks and springs. Collect the young, tender leaves throughout the year for a delicious meal, raw or cooked. They taste and cook much like spinach, and it makes a wonderful base for stir-fry or soup. Found in continental USA and in southern Canada but not North Dakota.

Wild Onion must smell like an onion, or it could be a toxic look-alike. Found NY, GA, TX-West, but not Oklahoma, Kansas, North Dakota, Nevada, or California. Found in southern Canada, but not Ontario.

Wild Rose is a thorny bush with fragrant, white-pink, 5-petaled, showy flowers May-July. Seed pods ripen orange red in August and remain good all winter. Petals make a good tea, can be added to salads, jellied, or candied. Rosehip juice has 6-24X more vitamin C than orange juice. Eaten fresh, some hips taste much like apples. They can be baked in breads or dried for teas.

Rose Hips are a vital source of vitamin C. Snap the stems and tails off and cook in just enough water to cover them, until well softened, and drain, press through a sieve, repeat—cook again with less water and strain through a sieve again. Discard skins and seeds, drain the remaining pulp in a fine cloth, preferably cheesecloth, use soon after since you don't have a refrigerator in which to store it. It doesn't have much taste but there is that vitamin C needed for good health. The remaining pulp can be spread thin and dried. When needed it can be pulverized, the powder sprinkled over cereal or in beverages, or used in place of a bit of flour in many other foods. Found in Continental USA and Canada except for Nunavut province.

Seeds are a good source of protein and can be winnowed and ground to a flour for baking, added to stews, roasted, or sprouted in a Ziplock with a bit of water added. Or they can be dried and stored for future use.

Wild fruits are among the largest classes of edible fruits. In some places it almost seems impossible for hunger to exist anywhere in the world with all the blackberries falling off the prickly canes. I've also picked pails of blueberries, winterberries, pin cherries, chokecherries, dewberries and grapes. I've found a cornucopia of wild food in an abandoned orchard in Mount Shasta with peaches, apples, prunes and plums, rhubarb on abandoned farmsteads, elderberry and serviceberry in the wild. I've picked black walnut and even English Walnut, butternut and hazelnut.

Although I've been very careful with the mushrooms, with a knowledgeable companion, Silvie, I gathered mushrooms in the Austrian Alps and recognized the safe Puffball in my parent's driveway in the woods of northern Minnesota. My mom was reluctant, but I sliced it and fried several delicious meals of it. I did the same with morels found in a nature park. Easily identified and delicious.

The pollen of the ubiquitous cattail is rich in protein. The slender head of the cattail can be harvested before the heads mature and eaten like sweet corn. The young shoots can be eaten in early spring and taste like celery, providing a useful source of carbohydrate. Rosehips, the fruit of wild roses, are an excellent source of vitamins A and C. Even the inner bark of trees, such as poplar, cottonwood, aspen, birch, and willow can be eaten in an emergency. The inner bark of pine palatable especially in spring, will provide vitamin C. The inner bark of young, new leaves of basswood and linden can be eaten as a salad.

The inner bark of slippery elm, pine trees, black birch, yellow birch, red spruce, black spruce, balsam fir, and tamarack can be harvested in spring when the bark is more easily removed from the tree trunk and the vitamin content is at its peak. If you take only narrow, vertical strips from the tree it will allow the tree to heal and be harvested again another year. Shave off the gray outer bark and the greenish middle bark to get to the rubbery cream-colored or white inner layer. Cut and peel off the white rubbery inner bark.

Dry the inner bark on a rack of tree branches or a flat rock, in the sun for about a day. You can eat it raw, fry or boil it in water to make bark snacks. To make bark flour dry it for a day, then pound it into a powder with a stone on a flat rock until it looks like oatmeal. To make bark bread, you'll need 2½ oz yeast or sour dough, 1 quart of water, 1 quart of rye flour, 1½ quarts of white flour, and ½ cup of bark flour, mixed in a bowl, stirred thoroughly, and set aside to rise about an hour, knead, sallow to rise again, roll out into 3" rounds, sprinkle with water before baking over hot coals, constantly turning until a baked crust develops—almost the way your great-great grand parents did it. Unless you didn't bring all that flour with you, you might want to get a jump start on growing it.

Growing Your Own

Be the first farmer in the rise of civilization from hunter-gatherer if you thought to bring a few wheat and spelt seeds on this micronova adventure. You'll have to start the first garden and grow it into a small wheat field, the first wheat field in your new civilization.

The first year you just clear the space and dig a shallow rectangular 3 x 6' hole, setting the soil aside. Gather vegetation and fill the hole with it. Sprinkle half of the soil over the top and plant your first garden, choosing the plants from the very hardy list below. Grow vegetables the first season and ⅓ of the garden in wheat to get enough seed to plant more the next year. Water and care for the first garden in this civilization. Shredded grass lightly spread over the soil can reduce drying of the soil. The next year make another 3 x 6' bed to grow more wheat and vegetables. Now you won't need to search for food as much, you'll be growing it near your new home. Here is a list of seeds you should bring in your survival kit. I selected plants that survived and grew well in the Pacific northwest garden that you should have in your survival garden and hopefully this is at least a place to begin to find plants that will grow best in the climate after Micronova.

***

Very Hardy 0°	**Hardy 10°**
Broccoli	Broccoli-Waltham
Brussels sprouts	Cabbage-Savoy
Cabbage (green)	Radish
Cauliflower	Rutabaga
Collards—vates	Fava Bean
Kale	Beets
Parsnip	Carrots
Chives	Celeriac
Garlic	Lettuce
Jerusalem Artichoke	New Zealand Spinach
Leeks	Rosemary
Horseradish	Florence Fennel
Onions—Walla Walla	
Peppermint	
Spearmint	
Spinach	
Sage	
Thyme	
Turnip	
Wintergreen	

Remember, there are no garden centers any longer, no seed catalogs. You must save seeds if you wish to grow a garden next year, or any year. That will require a good supply of Ziplock bags and save the packets to use as a marker to identify the seeds you've saved. Always use open-pollinated varieties so what you put in your future gardening kit will develop the same characteristics year after year. No hybrids in your future gardens—they don't breed true!

This is a combination of Mel Bartholomew's raised bed

gardening and Ruth Stout's Gardening without Work that I've been using and modifying for more than a decade before the Micronova and modified to account for a cooler climate Ben Davidson has predicted. We might wish that global warming was on its way, but that bubble has burst.

My recommendations to grow crops for a cooler climate with that in mind, opting for your best chance of success. Studies show a tendency toward cooler climate in the millennia ahead so better that you prepare for what will be instead of what you might like. Greenhouses could offer more choices, but glass will be out of reach of the technology of the new civilization and unless you can discover some intact windows, after the beating the Earth has taken from impactors and geological turmoil or the sturdier plastic sheets, gardening will be outdoors for a long time. Planting in a compost pile provides more warmth for the roots to get started in spring.

The layering of decaying plant material is intended to establish a natural warming from the compost pile on which you are gardening, and the carbon dioxide that is produced is a vital component of any growing system. Ruth did not set shovel to her ground as I suggested but she had time. You need food as immediately as possible. Digging down just three inches was intended more to provide a surface in which to plant since the stores in your area are no more and you can't buy a bag of compost. You must create it on the fly from materials at hand and with as little work and time as possible.

Growing your own food will give you an easier way to obtain food for you and your family than hunting and gathering, although gathering can include finding plants you can bring to your garden, some of them survivors or born of survivors like yourself. I wondered about the little red berries in the asparagus in my garden. Since these were fruits, there must be seeds. Would they sprout if I dried and then potted a few of them? I now have about 20 asparagus to plant in my garden to replace those I lost this past winter. If you find wild asparagus, you can collect the asparagus berries late in the season as well as the asparagus shoots early in the season. In spring, fiddlehead ferns are unrolling their leaves that rolled up and look like a fiddlehead. Peel away the wooly, rusty-looking skin at the base, wash and drain. Cook for about 5-8 minutes. If you have a bit of butter in your food kit, that tastes great melted over the fiddleheads—a gourmet meal to get your adventure kicked off in style. And you need chives in your garden.

Pemmican is a concentrated, nutritionally complete food invented by the plains Indians from dried bison meat and rendered fat prepared during dry months of summer. For early frontiersmen it became a food of choice because not only was it highly nutritious, but it would also remain safe to eat without refrigeration or other preservation processes for many years, as long as it was kept away from heat, moisture, and direct sunlight. Pemmican was solution to the hunger incurred in traveling or during lean winter months. Berries that were added for later recipes were for flavor, not as vital ingredients. And they increase the rate of spoilage without enhancing nutrition.

Pemmican is not a raw food. The fat must be heated above 200°F to get it out of the fatty tissue and rid it of moisture. The lean meat is dehydrated at temperatures below 120°F (100°F to 115°F is perfect). Above 120°F the meat is cooked and the nutritional value is lost. Federal and state laws no longer apply in this new civilization. You CAN make foods for survival in this new era you've now entered. Properly made pemmican can be eaten for months and years as your only food. All you need extra is drinking water. For the best pemmican use the red meat of deer, elk, bison. And the occasional wild cow that has been eating wild.

Use equal amounts of very dry meat and rendered beef tallow cooked in a pot that can set in a bed of coals for half a day or more, checking occasionally with a cooking thermometer. Add a bit more wood to your fire to keep the temperature around 240°F. When the cracklins are beginning to turn dark and most of them are chestnut brown take the roaster out of the coals. Put a cloth or paper towel in the strainer over a bowl and let it drain and then help it along by pressing down with a wooden spoon pour the contents of the pan into the strainer. Cracklins, with a bit of salt and pepper, can be eaten when cool enough. Save that liquid fat, let it cool. Fat of grass-fed animals has more Omega-3 fats that make this fat look somewhat orange because of the carotene from eating grass instead of grain. You're going to be eating healthier!

Cut the red meat into strips and dry until it's crispy. Pemmican is ½ fat and ½ dried meat. Any evidence of moisture will spoil, so look carefully for any lack of crispness. Bend the strips double to see if they crack or are rubbery. All should crack, any rubbery pieces are not ready to be included in your pemmican. Pound the dried strips into a powder with a clean rock on a clean flat rock. Add the shredded meat to an equal weight of fat and blend with a spoon—it should look like moist, crumbled brownies. Store in sandwich size Ziplock bags. That should be about 2,000 calories, set them aside to cool and harden. Store in a dark place at room temperature. Does not need refrigeration. Pemmican is unparalleled as a perfect food, calorie-dense and nutritionally complete.

Each person in your family should have a waterproof

bug out bag they can carry so the workload can be shared. You can't carry it all. You will need a little time to find a safe location.

Survival food for your backpack should, if possible, include Long Range Patrol Rations (LRPRs) which are freeze-dried meals that are also vacuum-packed, making them very light-weight, only 5 oz., needing only water to reconstitute. It should also include 2-4 bottles of drinking water, so you don't dehydrate before you get settled, a shelter built, fire started, and a solar still set up to extract water from damp soil. You'll find good uses for those empty containers, too. If you can manage to bring 1 gallon of water/day for each person you won't have to worry about dehydration for one day.

A basic toolkit would include a machete, small hatchet, folding camp shovel, a gun and ammo, hunting knives on a utility belt, folding pocketknives, a small fishing kit with hooks, line, and bobbers, tarps and rope, hammer, screwdrivers (Flat and Phillips) wrenches, crescent, pliers, tape measures, saws, small level, miscellaneous hardware fasteners, nails.

A poncho is a wise choice of survival clothing: it can be used as a makeshift tent, ground cloth, cover for sleeping bag or protection from ground moisture or dew. Be sure to include sturdy high-top shoes and extra socks, and head covering to protect you until the Earth's magnetosphere recovers to shield you from the cosmic rays, X-rays, and protons. Be sure the wardrobe you bring into the future is carefully selected to meet the needs of the coming Ice Age.

Your personal pack should be ready to go. Think of light, little things that are easy to carry, a needle and thread might be as life-saving as a pocketknife and poncho, folding shovel, folding camp saw. Prepping by watching a few survival videos while the technology is still available and functioning might be useful to learn skills, but to also get a few useful ideas for vital tools. Remember, you can't depend on your car for transportation. Gas stations or charging stations won't be operational. You need to be able to fend for yourself, find your own water, food, shelter.

Stay safe. Your brain is your fortress. This event will be extreme, but you CAN survive it—your ancestors did, back 12,000 years ago. You come from a long line of survivors!

The spirals danced and celebrated.
"He almost forgot the education he was getting by teaching all those youngsters about wild edible foods," smiled a Grandmother.
"And those boys he took camping on snowshoes in the winter," chortled a Grandfather. "It was part of his plan and he carried it out to perfection."
"That was a very wide-ranging agenda he set for himself," sighed the Dreamkeeper. "It required his professional life as well as much of his personal life."
"He found a way to make it all work toward completion of his agreement to return to warn his people that a train was on the tracks and that people needed to prepare for the micronova."

The End

Thank You For Reading!

Book 2 of the Quantum Dream Series

Surviving The Micronova:

This Train Is On The Tracks

https://allenheart.com

allen aslan heart

Acknowledgements

Larry Cloud Morgan (White Feather) taught me many things about Ojibway spirituality and opened the door to allow me to help young Ojibway college students and their professors rediscover some of their lost heritage at the Rediscovery Center, fulfilling part of the 7th Fire prophecy. Larry was an inspiration to many of his people as well as the light-skinned people who were searching for a new way of being—the Osh-ka-bi-ma-di-zig (the new people).

Josephine DeGroat was a loving traditional elder and support for Larry's task of bringing justice back to the reservation beclouded by corruption. She personally invited me to dance with her and the elders in the honors dance. She was also my source for the copy of the doctoral dissertation that revealed the historical basis for the Ojibway Dream Dance, and she distributed my booklets on the wisdom teachings of the 7th Fire Dreamcatcher Heritage Collection. Her lovingkindness is dearly missed and sweetly appreciated.

Bea Swanson, an elder on the board of Hunger Action Coalition, who I worked with in Loaves and Fishes, at St. Joseph's Catholic Church, bringing food to the people of the Little Earth community and who bravely confronted the white fishermen exploiting a treaty violation by the Minnesota governor.

Deanie Lerner was a close friend of both Larry and me and a great inspiration to let my playful, creative talents emerge, Hannah was a close friend to Larry, Deanie, and me, teaching me about healing and allowing me to heal her, and win her admiration.

Karan allowed me to do an awesome healing on her, shared a wonderful family with me, and went on to find a great normal guy to replace me. Frank NaSal was a wonderful guy to replace me and give Karan the stable, normal life she deserved. I taught my daughter, Kristin Becker, how to weave my dreamcatchers and she introduced these dream catchers to German-speaking Europe before I got there, got me to Europe 12 years ahead of time to see the Virgilskapelle so I was prepared to find it when I returned to Europe, and she became a naturopathic doctor which made me even more proud; my first daughter, Nicole, my sounding board for this book, who made me proud for her becoming an occupational therapist and lovingly helping so many people; Jeremy, son, who became a songwriter, singer and guitarist., a great Dad and deeply spiritual man.

Kay Ekwall learned to make exquisite dreamcatchers which we sold online around the world, drove me across country to help me teach dreamcatcher weaving and bravely shared a speaking engagement with me with the American Theosophical Society.

Madonna Gish not only requested a healing, but also asked me to contact her husband who had unexpectedly died, thereby setting up my only contact with the afterlife.

Hermine Knoll who suggested a name for us upon our marriage that was to help me direct the course of my life.

Ed and Ruth Ann Gehrke who, with Diane Joliquer and Barbara van Offeren introduced me to a modern-day approximation of a medieval mystery incubation rite underground, helping me understand the function of the Virgilskapelle and Magdalenskapelle.

Mishanagqus Vetrano provided a deep love and the extraordinary power of seeing what I could not see and shared a very short, but valuable time together before I left to teach where the pebble of ego-mind had been dropped into the ocean of consciousness.

Paul Pearsall left an enormous legacy in his great work before his untimely death in 2007.

Katje provided translation and shared her home and friends in a way that got me back to Vienna as well as Gertrude Stein who was vital in my return to Vienna to discover Magdalenskapelle in the history of Christianity.

Shari Fiksdal showed me her intuitive powers and awesome capacity to love, and probably the one who Mishanagqus saw as my intended partner.

Dianna Teachout called me to heal her horses and one of them whispered to me what the problem was. Noreen Teachout, her mom, provided a home base in Denver to saturate the dreamcatcher market there and where I received a commission from spirit to dance a new dream.

Harrald Purrier provided access to demonstrate dreamcatcher weaving, talk to Aztec dancers between their performances and get invited to repeat that in Vienna.

Sylvie Schrott arranged a second journey for me to Europe to teach her students about dreamcatchers, suggested I go to the esoteric convention in her town and provided a base to market dreamcatchers in Europe, got her ex-boyfriend's camper to drive us to markets in Germany, Netherlands, and Switzerland which got me a gig at a Swiss powwow, brought me to the local Geburtshaus that revealed the probable use of the twin chapels in Vienna. She helped arrange connections to the Stein workshop, as suggested by one of her friends, translated my dreamcatcher story tags and catalogs into German, invited me to travel to Slovenia with her which opened Slovenia to more presentations, including a 3-hour radio interview on Radio Pirhan broadcast to the Adriatic Sea community and so much more.

Karin was a wonderful translator and guide in Slovenia.

Orea got me started doing healing and launched a new spiritual perspective on life.

Mindy Shafer received my view of Minnesota farmscapes 30 years before she was born, showing the evidence that confirmed the scientific work of Dr, Paul Pearsall in his book, *The Heart's Code*.

Rosemary Herrold asked me to come to Chicago to do healing work on her which opened the opportunity to teach in Chicago and suburbs.

Mary Louise Hunt-Smith invited me to journey with her to a family Christmas in Texas which launched my adventure outside Minnesota, and to a family gathering in Mexico in which my near-drowning led to my experience of being saved by two "angels" who were employed as lifeguards. Then she found a job for both of us in a mobile home park that provided an income for both of us managing and living in an awesome home that was on the National Historical Register, the manager's residence which provided a home base to set up classes all around the Twin Cities of Minneapolis and St. Paul. She also identified elements of A Course in Miracles in my work even though I had never heard of it at that time. She would occasionally complain to me that I seemed to be attuned to those teachings and had never read about it whereas she had studied and taught ACIM for 30 years.

Linda urged me to take art instruction workshop with Arthur Douet, brought me to the Brian Swimme documentary, arranged for three of us to present my resulting poem, 'I Am a Child of God's Universe' at the Noetic Institute in San Francisco and in a New Year's Eve prayer for a pray for peace rally.

Shirley Roden recommended my dreamcatcher presentation to the organizers of the annual workshop at Gaunt's House in Dorset, England, broadening my outreach.

Ed and Ruth Ann built the underground facility to support the teaching of a simplified, modernized, mystic rite of incubation facility. Barbara van Offeren brought an invitation for me to see this mystic group off to Australia for a monthlong walkabout and to welcome them back when they returned.

Another Barbara invited me to Australia to a different sort of walkabout that included a ride through an Indonesian jungle on an elephant and a visit to the Flinders Range to see the Aboriginal rock art.

There are many more I might have forgotten but 80 years can be a rather long time to remember names, events, and the details of their role in this far flung, rambling adventure on 4 continents.

allen aslan heart—Custer, WA.

About Allen Aslan Heart

I AM White Eagle Soaring, bridging the worlds of spirit and science. I was born on August 1st, 1941. I AM teacher and learner, of European descent and Native American. I have spoken at Unitarian, Unity, and Religious Science churches across the USA, as well as classes on topics from Natural Lawn Care and Natural Therapies for ADD, to Dreamcatcher Wisdom Teachings and Dreamcatcher Weaving. Radio Pirhan broadcast in region of the Adriatic Sea, in Museums, Adult Education, Public Libraries, and to organizations such as United Nations Vienna, Vienna-American International School, and the Theosophical Society HQ in Wheaton, IL.

I didn't choose dreamcatchers, they chose me. I didn't plan to leave my comfortable job teaching science in the public schools. I didn't plan to listen to the sissagwad, the soft wind of spirit, or weave dreamcatchers and tell their stories. Instead dreamcatchers wove me through the soft whispers of the Grandmothers and Grandfathers, to change a skeptic into a shaman, showing me a path of wonder and wisdom I couldn't have imagined, to discover the real and powerful synthesis between science and spirit.

Bibliography

Key To Citations:

OS= Observer Supplement
NEW= Next End of the Earth
GDJ= God's Day Of Judgement
SFB= Shamanism for Beginners
POG=Physics of God
POH=Proof of Heaven

Alexander, Eben, MD. Proof of Heaven: A Neurosurgeon's Journey Into The Afterlife. New York: Simon & Schuster, 2012.
Alexander, Eben and Ptolemy Tompkins. The Map of Heaven: How Science, Religion, and Ordinary People Are Proving the Afterlife. New York: Simon & Schuster, 2014.
Alexander, Eben and Karen Newell. Living in a Mindful Universe: A Neurosurgeon's Journey into the Heart of Consciousness. New York: Rodale, 2017.
Baigent, Michael. The Jesus Papers: Exposing the Greatest Cover-Up in History. New York: Harper Collins, 2006.
Bartholomew, Mel. Square Foot Gardening. Emmaus PA: Rodale Books, 1981.
Bartholomew, Mel. All New Square Foot Gardening: Grow More in Less Space. Brentwood TN: Cool Springs Press, 2006.
Brown, Tom, Jr. , with Brandt Morgan. Tom Brown's Field Guide to Living with the Earth. New York: Berkley Books, 1984.
Cain, Alexander. Alive after the Fall.2020.
Campbell, Stu. Let It Rot: The Gardener's Guide to Composting. Pownal Vermont: Storey Communications, 1990, 1975.
Campbell, Stu. Mulch It! A practical guide to using mulch in the garden and landscape. North Adams MA: Storey Communications, 2001.
Capra, Fritjof. The Tao of Physics: An Exploration of the Parallels between Modern Physics and Eastern Mysticism. Berkeley CA: Shambala Publications, 1975.
Cech, Richo. Making Plant Medicine. Williams OR: Horizon Herbs, 2000.
Collins, Andrew. The Cygnus Key: The Denisovan Legacy, Gobekli Tepe, and the Birth of Egypt. Rochester VT: Bear & Co., 2018.
Collins, Andrew and Gregory L. Little. Denisovan Origins: Hybrid Humans, Gobekli Tepe, and the Genesis of the Giants of Ancient America. Rochester VT: Bear & Co., 2019.
Dalrymple, Byron. The Outdoor Emergency Survival Guide. USA. 1987.
Davidovits, Joseph. Why the Pharaohs Built the Pyramids with Fake Stones: The Ultimate Scientific Proofs, The Rise and Decline of a Technology. Saint-Quentin, France: Institut Geopolymere, 2009.
Davidson, Ben. The Next End of the Earth; the Rebirth of Catastrophism.

Colorado Springs: Space Weather News, 2021. Colorado Springs: Space Weather News, 2022.

Davidson, Ben. Observer Supplement, 2022-2023: Solar-Terrestrial Physics & Modern Catastrophism. Colorado Springs: Space Weather News, 2022.

Davidson, Ben. Weatherman's Guide to the Sun, 3rd Ed. Colorado Springs: Space Weather News, 2022.

Davies, Paul. God and the New Physics. New York: Simon & Schuster, 1983.

Davis, Claude. The Lost Ways. www.askaprepper.com. 2017.

Dossey, Larry. The Science of Premonitions: How Knowing the Future Can Help Us Avoid Danger, Maximize Opportunities, and Create a Better Life. New York: Plume, 2010.

Drake, Michael. The Shamanic Drum. A Guide to Shamanic Drumming, A Guide to Sacred Drumming. Goldendale WA: Talkingdrum Publications, 1991.

Feynman, Richard. Six Not-So Easy Pieces: Einstein's Relativity, Symmetry, and Space-Time. Cambridge MA: Perseus Books, 1997.

Duke, James, A. PhD. The Green Pharmacy: New Discoveries in Herbal Remedies for Common Diseases and Conditions from the World's Foremost Authority on Healing Herbs. Emmaus PA: Rodale Books, 1997.

Faulkner, Edward. Plowman's Folly. New York: Grosset & Dunlap, 1943.

Freke, Timothy and Peter Gandy. Jesus and the Lost Goddess, The Secret Teachings of the Original Christians. New York: Harmony Books, 2001.

Freke, Timothy and Peter Gandy. The Laughing Jesus: Religious Lies and Gnostic Wisdom. New York: Three Rivers Press, 2005.

Freke, Timothy and Peter Gandy. The Jesus Mysteries: Was the 'Original Jesus' a Pagan God? New York: Three Rivers Press, 2005.

Furlong, Marjorie and Virginia Pill. Wild Edible Fruits & Berries. Healdsburg CA: Naturegraph Publishers, 1974.

Goldbloom, Shelley. Garden Smarts: A Bounty of Tips from North American's Best Gardeners. Old Saybrook CT: The Globe Pequot Press, 1995, 1993.

Goswami, Amit. The Self-Aware Universe. New York: Putnam's Sons, 1993.

Greyson, Bruce, M.D. After: A Doctor Explores What Near-Death Experiences Reveal about Life and Beyond. NY: St. Martin's, 2021.

Griffin, Thomas H. Back Trail Cooking: A Practical Guide to the Planning and Preparation of Backpack Foods for Both the Inexperienced and Seasoned Backpacker. Ramona CA: Sentinel Publications, 1970.

Gullett, Walt &Jane Fellows Gullett. Everyone's Guide to Food Self-Sufficiency. Happy Camp CA: Naturegraph, 1981.

Hancock, Graham. Fingerprints of the Gods: The Evidence of Earth's Lost Civilization. New York: Crown, 1995.

Harrison, John Bede. Growing Food Organically. West Vancouver, Canada: Waterwheel Press, 1993.

Hurdle, J. Frank, M.D. A Country Doctor's Common-Sense Manual. West Nyack NY: Parker Publishing, 1975.

Jung, Carl G. Man and His Symbols. Garden City NY: Doubleday, 1964.

Kelly, Penny. Consciousness and Energy, Volume 1. Lawton MI: Lily Hill

Publishing, 2006.
Kelly, Penny with William C. Levengood, Consciousness and Energy, Volume 2: New Worlds of Energy. Lawton MI: Lily Hill Publishing, 2012.
Kelly, Penny. Consciousness and Energy, Volume 3, Religion, Sex, Power and the Fall of Consciousness. Lawton MI: Lily Hill Publishing, 2015.
Kelly, Penny. Consciousness and Energy, Volume 4: Trump, the Sting, the Catastrophe Cycle and Consciousness. Lawton MI: Lily Hill Publishing, 2006.
Kelly, Edward F. and Emily Williams Kelly, et al. Irreducible Mind, Toward a Psychology for the 21st Century. Lanham MD: Rowman & Littlefield: 2010.03
Kerrod, Robin. The Star Guide: Learn How To Read the Night Sky Star by Star. NY: Macmillan: 1991.
King James Version of The Holy Bible. London, 1611.
LaViolette, Paul, PhD. Genesis of the Cosmos: The Ancient Science of Continuous Creation Rochester, VT: Bear & Co., 2004.
McGlashan, Charles F. History of the Donner Party, A Tragedy of the Sierra. Truckee, CA: Overland Journeys to the Pacific Publishers. 1879.
Mack, Norman, ed. Back to Basics: How to Learn and Enjoy Traditional American Skills. Pleasantville, NY: Reader's Digest Association, Inc., 1981.
Niemeyer, Roy K. Beginning Archery. Belmont CA: Wadsworth, 1969.
Ortberg, John. Eternity Is Now in Session: A Radical Rediscovery of What Jesus Really Taught about Salvation, Eternity, and Getting to the Good Place. Carol Stream IL: Tyndale House Publishers, 2015.
Paddison, Sara. The Hidden Power of the Heart. Boulder Creek CA: Planetary Publications, 1992.
Pearsall, Paul A. The Heart's Code: Tapping the Wisdom and Power of our Heart Energy. New York: Broadway Books, 1998.
Rajneesh, Bagwan Shree. Meditation: The First and Last Freedom. The Rebel Publishing House, Cologne Germany, undated.
Ratcliffe, Martin and Charles Nix. The Night Sky Deck. NY: Barnes & Noble, 2005.
Rosenblum, Bruce and Fred Kuttner. Quantum Enigma: Physics Encounters Consciousness. Oxford NY: Oxford University Press, 2011.
Sapphire. Mastering Remote Viewing: Remote Viewing, Third Eye & Astral Projection: Sapphire, 2006-7.
Schoch, Robert M., Ph.D. and Robert Aquinas McNally. Voices of the Rocks: A Scientist Looks at Catastrophes and Ancient Civilizations. New York: Harmony Books, 1999.
Schwartz, Gary E.R., Ph.D. and Linda G S Russek, PhD. The Living Universe: a fundamental discovery that transforms science and medicine. Charlottesville VA: Hampton Roads, 1999.
Selbie, Joseph. The Physics of God: How the Deepest Theories of Science Explain Religion and How the Deepest Truths of Religion Explain Science. New Newburyport MA: New Page Books, 2021.
Shanks, Bernard. Wilderness Survival, revised edition. New York: Universe Books, 1980,1987.
Shane, Adolph. Archery Tackle: How to make and Use It. Azle TX, Bois d'Arc

Press, 1990;1936.
Silva, Mari. Shamanism for Beginners: The Ultimate Beginner's Guide to Walking the Path of the Shaman, Shamanic Journeying and Raising Consciousness. https://spiritualityspot.com. 2021.
Stone, Justin. T'ai Chi Chih!: Joy Thru Movement. San Luis Obispo CA: Sun Publishing, 1980.
Stout, Ruth. How to Have a Green Thumb Without an Aching Back: A New Method of Mulch Gardening. New York: Cornerstone Library, 1975, 1973, 1968, 1955.
Stout, Ruth. Gardening Without Work. Emmaus PA: Rodale Books. 1960.
Swimme, Brian. The Universe is a Green Dragon: A Cosmic Creation Story. Santa Fe: Bear & Co., 1984.
van Lommel, Pim. Consciousness Beyond Life: The Science of the Near-Death Experience. NY: HarperCollins, 2010.
Velikovsky, Immanuel. Worlds in Collision. New York: Macmillan, 1950.
Velikovsky, Immanuel. Earth in Upheaval. Garden City: Doubleday, 1977.
Vogt, Douglas B. God's Day of Judgment: The Real Cause of Global Warming. Jacksonville, FL: Vector Associates, 2007.
Vogt, Douglas B. The Theory of Multidimensional Reality: The Only Information Theory of Existence. Jacksonville, FL: Vector Associates, 2015.
Weinberg, Steven. Dreams of a Final Theory. New York: Vintage Books, 1994.
Wigginton, Eliot. The Foxfire Book: Hog dressing; log cabin building; mountain crafts and foods; planting by the signs; snake lore, hunting tales; faith healing; moonshining; and other affairs of plain living. Garden City NY: Anchor Books, 1972.
Zukav, Gary. The Dancing Wu Li Masters: An Overview of the New Physics. New York: William Morrow, 1979.

Book 1 in the Quantum Dream Series

Dancing A Quantum Dream

An 80 Year Journey of Initiation, Quiet Miracles, Teaching and Shamanic Communications

Surviving The Micronova

This Train Is On The Tracks

Book 2 in the Quantum Dream Series

by allen aslan heart

Printed in Great Britain
by Amazon